MW00880128

Through Asia

A WHISPER FROM THE EAST

TAM HUY NGUYEN

Library of Congress Control Number: 2020904363
ISBN: Hardcover   978-1-7960-9172-4
               Softcover   978-1-7960-9171-7
               eBook   978-1-7960-9170-0

Author: Tam Huy Nguyen
Translator: Khanh Truong
Editor: Alice Nguyen
Cover Illustrator: Eric Nguyen
Layout Illustrator: Van Vu

Print information available on the last page.

Rev. date: 03/02/2020

To order additional copies of this book, contact:
Xlibris
1-888-795-4274
www.Xlibris.com
Orders@Xlibris.com
810557

Contents

Thank you to all the roads I walked

and all the faces I met...

INTRODUCTION

Warning: This is not a travel guide

That's right! From here until the very end of this book, you will not be able to find a guide or any possible itinerary. But one thing is for sure: there is a motivation in here – motivation to make you rush to the internet, find a flight comparison site, log into travel forum to look for a mate, or sign up for Couchsurfing to find a host who is willing to let you stay with them in some corner of the world.

For me, there is always an overwhelming feeling of anticipation every time I stand with my backpack in the middle of a strange place, so much happiness that I feel breathless. Being able to go, to experience, and to dive in an existing place and culture is a joy already. And "Happiness is only real when shared," right?

This book does not cultivate in you any considerable thinking or transmit any sublime philosophy. The only tool used in this book are the truthfulness of stories, the stir about the bigness of the world, the desire to step outside with a thirsty heart and thoughts to explore, and the experience which is completely my own.

Yes, this is simply the journey of a romantic guy who wandered alone across cities. From the first day I stepped out, gawky and trembling, into the Asian metropolises of Singapore, Bangkok, Siem Reap, Hong Kong and others to the days when I found myself crazily alone in the midst of a European white winter in places like Paris, Venice, Zurich and Milan.

And then there were the long days when my backpack and I dragged each other across sun-down deserts to place my footprints in luxurious American havens like Los Angeles, New York, Washington DC and Las Vegas. Or the days I stood in awe of the beauty of hundred-year-old temples in places like Tokyo, Luang Prabang, Kyoto, and Bagan.

On my own with the backpack, I followed peaceful Asian routes, travelled on European express trains, and took cheap flights over high-living American cities. Each city bears different stories, different feelings and a different milestone of personal maturity. I may have been all alone, but I was not lonely. On each path I took, I met friends who shared the same direction. They, from a smorgasbord of nationalities – Moroccan, German, Swiss, Norwegian, Russian, South African, Malaysian, Hong Kong, Australian, Chinese, Canadian – and of course, my fellow Vietnamese countrymen – helped me wherever I found myself. Together we explored the world.

And my journeys throughout the cities of the world definitely do not end here. By the time this book reaches your hand, I will still be sniffing around for cheap flights. To where? How about mysterious cities in Africa? Maybe the far distant South America? Somewhere cold in Eastern Europe is not a bad option either. It could be any city which I have never seen. As you can see, I am not a guy with a solid plan...

One day, if you figure out for yourself that you too are a city-hopping nomad, you may have your own mission to conquer the roads that lead you into the big, big world. The destinations themselves may not be as important as the journeys. Less thinking, less doubt, less fear, less worry about judgment. Just go, and there will be a way...

As an Asian, before stepping out into
the world, you must cross Asia.

I used to look at my Western friends eagerly traveling around Asia,
and I would wonder why they were so enthusiastic. While I, though
living in the middle of Asia, wasn't interested. While in my dreams,
my ambition was for Paris, for Venice, for New York... as soon as those
captivating places went through my head, I'd immediately label them
as "Dreams for fun." And because they were just for fun, they should be
as ambitious as they could be!

Who could tax my dreams, the dreams of an ordinary guy with an
ordinary family background, ordinary education, and ordinary job?
Every morning, I would wake up and neither a foreign scholarship nor
lottery jackpot would drop on my head. The world out there is massively
big, I would think to myself, how can I possibly touch it? Then I gave
myself an answer: perhaps it would be impossible to travel to those dream
cities, but why not somewhere nearby? It is usually said, "Just go and
there will be a way", right? I had no idea where I would go, but Sai Gon
felt smaller and smaller against my desire to explore the world. Toddling
on unsteady feet, I took my first steps, starting from the cities of my own
Asian continent.

Little by little, I came to understand why Westerners spend months
or even years wandering around Asian routes. I've learned that those
destinations could be so special, so inscrutable, so strange, so challenging
as well as so beautiful, so splendid and so... Asian. Each city has different

stories, a different soul, different whispers telling you its proud past, present and future.

This journey did not just happen; it's not just an overnight story. It's been a tireless, unfolding tale that's taken years. So, there's no need to rush, dear reader. Take your time, read it slowly, feel your way along, bit by bit. I will tell you my story about a slow and leisurely Asia, about my first steps in unfamiliar cities. Without this start, I would not have gone anywhere...

PART I

SOUTHEAST ASIA HOMELAND LULLABY

CHAPTER 1

———

MYANMAR
WHERE CITIES REFUSED
TO WAKE UP

In this life, when it is still possible, many people would just wake up in the morning, go to work until late in the afternoon. Mornings, noons, afternoons, evenings or even late evenings before going to bed, I still heard people moaning, including me, that "Life is so hard", "Life is suffering". But, whenever I recall the magically tranquil eyes and calm faces of people I met in Myanmar, I would like to be them, I would choose to live the way they live. That is, to be equanimous facing matters. Every person we met would teach us good lessons. But this was the first time when I was taught that Happiness has nothing to do with Poverty or Wealth.

BAGAN
THE SOUND OF HORSE'S
HOOFS AT DUSK

———

There were tens of ways to go to Bagan, hundreds of articles about Bagan, thousands of praises for Bagan. But there was only one thing that obsessed me about Bagan after all the other things more or less faded with time, that was the sounds of horse hooves in twilight Bagan when the darkness covered temples little by little ...

It was the end of summer, when rains made way for flourishing shoots on vast fields. It was said that this area would be decertified and may become a second Sahara. But it didn't happen that way, not at all. There were still shady roads, newly-seeded bean patches, and palm trees rising high to the sky. On that green ground, more than three thousand red-brick temples adorned the whole area creating a scene that was majestic and yet melancholy. If being asked what I search in Bagan, I would say I search for peace.

Yes, away from noise and rush, from cities rapidly developing, Bagan was like a small dot where we could find balance for the soul. Go there once, to know that it is so easy to fall in love for a strange place.

The night bus from Yangon arrived Bagan at five in the morning, when everything was still in the dim light of early morning, ready to start a new day. We tiredly got on a minivan to go to the center. The driver asked:

"So, there are three areas, one with fancy hotels, one is Nyaung-U with cheap hostels and the Old Bagan which is extremely expensive, where do you want?"

I, although sleepy, was still awake enough to choose the cheap area.

You know, I was backpacking, I did not have enough budget to stay in a fancy hotel anyway. Also, there would be many many backpackers from all the world who would stay in cheap places, it would be a great opportunity to make friends, sound interesting, right? If you choose to be a nomad, getting to know new people is important.

The bus went into the dark road ahead. I heard the rhythmic horse hooves knocking on the road somewhere. It was the first time I heard that sound, far and near...

In the vague light of early morning on the way, I saw a Korean couple cycling to the direction of the sun. they were side by side, giving me a feeling of peace and simplicity. "They are watching the sunrise", the driver explained to me. Didn't know why, but it made me completely forget the tiredness after the night bus, forget the desire to rest my back a bit on a bed, I just wanted to rush to those abandoned temples. "Bagan, the legendary Bagan, here I am!". Just a little bit more, for sure I would be standing high on a temple, taking a panoramic view of everything around with an immense astonishment.

The morning in this small Nyaung-U, just stepping out and we could see several horse carts waiting for passengers, the whole town was deep in tranquility. At a time, Bagan was a huge area of 104-kilometer square with over three thousand temples and shrines that stretch out as far as the eye could see. Due to earthquakes and influences of time, there are now only about 1,500 ones left and remained intact. I could have opted to rent a bicycle or e-bike or taxi or bus to explore but I chose a horse cart right away driven by a small and smiling man. What could be better than riding on a horse cart in a clear morning when the sun pouring down its honey-like golden sunshine rhythmed by the clatter of chariot wheels on the shady road.

My first day in Bagan started with a cup of milk tea in local style and the good-smelly yummy noodle. At the opposite of the road, the Shwezigon pagoda shone gloriously under the early sunshine. Undeniably, this pagoda would open the door to any fanciful journeys in this legendary Bagan. Why? Because right at the moment you stepped into the place built in 1102, all your sorrow and troubles seemed to melt away. The morning chants rang in the breeze, the pray of a heartfelt woman in front of the principal altar, the twitter of sparrows, the tinkle of windchimes, the sound of the sun shining on leaf blades, even peace made sounds, slowly and elegantly. I offered flowers to the Buddha praying health for my mother, family and friends. I completely forgot that just one day before I still ran like hell in Kuala Lumpur Airport, squeezed myself to get over the traffic jam in Saigon, still had a heavy brain of nonsense stuff. At this very moment, my mind was completely quiet and peaceful. It was the feeling during the whole trip. Quiet and peace, quiet and peace…

The clatter of chariot wheels on asphalted roads sounded pleasant to the ears, like the sound of victory. After moving across cities, taking buses in Gulf of Thailand, flying over American cities, taking trains in Europe, falling asleep on cars in strange cities, but this was the first time I rode on a horse cart to explore a place. Trust me, if you were standing in the middle of Bagan temples, engine vehicles would become strangely inappropriate, they would be so wrong. The noise of motorbikes, buses or cars would become out of the place and ridiculous in this religious atmosphere. And in the middle of that majestic scene, peace became the only sound that existed. And human, the trouble makers, should only come there by bicycle, e-bikes, horse carts, or walking. Getting there slowly, then being swallowed slowly by the holy peace…

Bagan after thousands of years was still as intact as yesterday. I've been to Ananda Temple, Dhammayangyi Temple, Dhammayazika Pagoda, Gawdawpalin Temple, Gubyaukgyi Temple, Htilominlo Temple, Payathonzu Temple, Tharabha Gate, Thatbyinnyu Temple, etc. Can't remember them all, can't even read their names fully. Of all these thousands of temples and shrines, there were ones which were huge and beautiful mostly visited, yet there were ones which was just quietly located by the side of the road. For sure, they all have their names, their stories, and happiness and sorrows after times. But to me, forever, they all have one unique name: Bagan – the land where even the breath of the earth is also peaceful.

The horse-cart coachman drove us to almost most-famous places in Bagan. I was so moved when touching paintings by bare hand in a pagoda with one thousand years old, when walking along the deep hallways with majestic and solemn Buddha statues and faithful people kneeling at His feet. Looking at the woman holding her mala whispering chants or the man meticulously inlaying the statue with gold, I felt all scrambles for fame and wealth and social envies were left far behind the door, over the river, or as far as the distance of a flight or a whole day travelling by bus. It didn't matter how far they were, but one thing for sure during days in Bagan: none of those bad things could squeeze into our minds.

My friends said: Thanks for bringing them here, to live days of worry-free. And to realize that we had wasted too many days before for sadness and sorrows...

And thus, from morning with the sun shining to noon with meals in a local place, then afternoon on horse carts passing red-soil roads, I lived through days with thick atmosphere of peace, in the sound of the horse hooves...

In the afternoon, when the sun nearly went down behind the mountains, I told the horse-cart coachman to bring us to a perfect spot for sunset. There are two specialties in Bagan which everyone would want to see: sunrise and sunset. When the sun was in the fine line between the brightness and darkness, temples and shrines would become very illusory. On a high position, there were already many tourists sitting still unable to take their eyes off the sun setting down slowly behind the mountains. I learnt this way of enjoying when I was in Siem Reap, following the flow of people climbing up to the hill to watch sunset. Then Fuji Mount in Tokyo, then Luang Prabang in Laos. Just like when it was twilight, when everybody took off their masks and layers of makeup, "La vita è bella". Same analogue.

However, watching sunset (or sunrise) is a matter of luck. Just a cloud covers, the whole waiting would become meaningless. The regret after climbing up only to know that you have missed something which is very, very beautiful may be not too different from a broken heart. Luckily, in another afternoon, while on a bus leaving Bagan, the sky became glamorous, shining all the majestic temples against the orange sky. To people who are living in busy cities, this is insane: unreal and speechless.

When the sun already set behind the far far away mountains, we all got on the horse cart back to Nang-U town. The darkness was ahead while the temples was left behind along the quiet lines of trees in the monotonous sound of horse hooves… clip-clop clip-clop… Those were the days in Bagan, everything was a bit of blur, only that clip clopping sound went into our peaceful sleeps… Trust me, no one would ever leave Bagan without being obsessed by the sound, no one!

THE LAND OF THE HAPPINESS

———

After days in Myanmar, everything – emotions, sceneries and people – was all overfilled yet I hardly found an adjective to say about it. There was something that is very unique, very different from all what I have seen in other places, things that cannot be named.

It was in a morning of gentle rain, when Nyaungshwe town turned into deeply green under the rain which lasted until midnight. (Well, the truth is: it's not easy to read and to remember names in Myanmar, at least to me). I walked to the boat jetty sharing same umbrella with an old man. He was dark-skinned wearing a worn-out shirt and a longyi which was not much better. Many people looked at me and waved on the way. They may know that I was tourist, or at least if I was walking with him, high chance was a tourist. I also waved back to them and put on the biggest smile I could have. Being friendly is always good while travelling. Then the old man said: "Myanmar is poor, but we are always happy!". I was suddenly frozen. Happy, Happiness – that is the WORD. It was the one that I was looking for to describe this country. From taxi drivers, horse cart coachmen, to girls selling stuff, hostel owners or even room service staff. They always smile joyfully. Many questions popped up in my head in that moment and they were all about Poverty and Happiness. Could it be?

Well, Why Not! IT COULD BE.

I usually self-satirize that I have enough – enough clothes, enough food. If I want to buy something which is not ridiculously expensive, I spend no time to ponder. I may not be a rich guy, but I have enough justification to call myself happy. That means Happiness is a concept that follows material values. It sounds like a fact that would never change. Yet, in that morning, on that reddy muddy road, a poor boatman who ferried tourists across Inle lake enlightened me about the definition of happiness. There was nothing of Ah Q spirit in what he said. Poverty and happiness seemed to be on two different roads, not related to each other. It just meant that whether being poor or wealthy, happiness is not the result of any previous action or state. Happy means happy, that is it!

Like the young boy who guided me around Inle lake. The boat ran the whole day, dropped by here and there. He waited for me outside, always ready to go to next stop. His kind smile was always there, yet absolutely silent. The silence like the still lake in afternoon. He was always quiet doing his job carefully, giving zero annoying look at me if I did not buy anything from souvenir stores along the lake (the look of tourist guides), as well as he never poked his nose into any conversations between me and my friends. It was like there were only us on the boat, he and the boat were just the vehicle touring us around. However, he did understand everything I said, he planned a great schedule smartly, delivered neat and clear answers to everything I asked. The rest was his silence. When I expressed that I wanted to go back a bit late so that I could watch sunset on the lake, he stopped the boat in the middle, leaving it drifting slowly. This made me realize that he would be able to go home earlier if we did not want such. The boat was still floating in the middle of the lake, ignoring waves lapping to the boat sides after each boats passing by. Or when we saw the rain was coming, I said we should go home, then he sped up, after a nod of head, he again went back to his job, patiently. Not a single emotion on his face. If our soul can just be like this still water, then, how happy we can be!

Or like the souvenir girl in a pagoda. When I arrived, she showed me the way to a belvedere hilltop. From there, I could have a panorama view of the pagoda, and Bagan appeared beautifully. She just stood there quietly, and helped tourists take photos when they needed. That was all. And she rejected the money I gave as a thank. I was so surprised. So why they did that job? What for? Why they didn't take the money? When I asked why, she said she brought me here not for money, so she would not take it. But she had a souvenir store, so if I liked, I could buy some from her. If not, then it was ok, no problem. "No problem" – the word that always brings me peace whenever travelling. I could buy some, or I could buy nothing. But that girl still brought tourists to the hilltop and received no money. She stood quietly in a corner, no inviting with insistence, no complaining, no forcing; she always kindly smiled. I wish that she can just keep on that, in that thousand-year pagoda. I wish her smile can be that kind and nice, forever.

Money is important, of course. But in Myanmar, there is something else that is more important. That is Happiness. Yes, people are not just all about money. They always laugh happily. Over a week staying there, going to many places, I never heard anyone pick a quarrel with someone else...

The hostel owner furtively took a photo of me with her Galaxy Tab. I asked if she wanted a picture of mine, let me smile to have a good one. She was so happy and explained that she saved photos of cute guests who stayed in her hostel. Then I grabbed Tiha and Lele, the two room attendants who were one-head shorter than me with dark skin and were always shy. The owner lady was a bit brighter than others - she looked like being born in a rich family, up-to-date with a Samsung Tab on hand and very good English. I told Hien (my friend) to pay more money, because she let us do early check-in – 10 hours earlier than regular – and late checkout – we had to wait for the bus, we even used a lot of water for shower before leaving – for FREE. Myanmar was not a rich country; I didn't want to presume on their kind nature. I simply thought: if I used anything, I would pay for it; electricity, water, food, room service, etc. they were money. She asked us what the money was for.

"We did early check-in and late check-out. However, it is not the point, the point is we want to thank you and the two girls for treating us so well during the time we were here", we explained.

But she didn't take it. She said, they didn't do that for money, so we shouldn't have thought that way.

"If you want to thank, recommend more Vietnamese guests for us. We would appreciate."

Nevertheless, we already determined to pay that money, so I gave to the two girls. But they firmly refused to receive, by all means. And when they refused my money, their eyes were sparkling without any hesitation. Well, that was it. No matter who they were, they didn't do anything to earn money. I didn't know why they did so to me, maybe because I always made them laugh? Or always complimented on their food? Applied Thanaka beautifully and always spent time to talk to them and know more about them? And between happiness and money, they chose the former, even though they deserved the money.

I asked Tiha "Why don't take my money? It's how we thank you."

"I work here and get paid. Talking to you is fun. And that is more important than money." She replied. "You are leaving here soon, don't forget us, huh? Next time you visit, take my bike. No need to rent one."

I was so moved, and promised that I would not forget them. And pretty sure that in my poor memory, their names would be carefully saved. Even though they were just random people I met, still, there were something forever inscribed.

The moment we left, the owner and Tiha and Lele all stood in front of the hostel to see our bus leaving Bagan. Before turing to a different road, I still saw those waving hands...

In this life, when it is still possible, many people would just wake up in the morning, go to work until late in the afternoon. Mornings, noons, afternoons, evenings or even late evenings before going to bed, I still heard people moaning, including me, that "Life is so hard" "Life is suffering". But, whenever I recall the magically tranquil eyes and calm faces of people I met in Myanmar, I would like to be them, I would choose to live the way they live. That is, to be equanimous facing matters. Every person we met would teach us good lesson. But this was the first time when I was taught that Happiness has nothing to do with Poverty or Wealth. I still can see kind peaceful smiles and happy faces of those rough-looking people whenever I think of those wandering days in that magic land. Myanmar, land of happiness, the place where everybody has happiness in their gene...

CHAPTER 2

CAMERON HIGHLAND
THE HIGHLAND AT ITS PEACE

There was a place which was somewhere among endless mountains, may take some kilometers just for dinners. At night when it was a bit chilly, sitting at a Starbucks, listening to the sounds of English, Chinese, Malaysian and felt like being in a suburb of a European city. Song – my friend – said, "I thought I were in England?". I myself thought I must have been in Switzerland. It was really the same. It gave me the exact feeling like what I felt when I was in Damiano's small village when we rode to Lugano at night for a mojito. I really love this place, a little peace for my little heart…

Ryan's house

Ryan sent me a Couchsurfing request, "In two weeks, I would fly from Kuala Lumpur to Vietnam and stay for four days. I already booked my hotel, I just wanna know if you feel like hanging out with me having coffee and discovering local food if you have time?". Well, I could do nothing better than this. I suddenly remembered I would fly to KL next week, that meant Ryan would have chance to show me his good will first, when I visited his city. I replied to him and told him my plan. However, Ryan sent me another reply in pity explaining that next week would be the election in Malaysia, he must be in his hometown to vote. I asked where his hometown was. He said Cameron Highland. Speechless. I asked if I could join him to his hometown because it was where I wanted to go but not yet figured out how to get there. Of course, Ryan agreed but he added "my house is poor, if you don't ask for high standards, then it should be ok". Well, I never cared about facilities. He could live with it, so did I. Therefore, by default, I travelled to Cameron Highland with a local. Yay!

I asked him: "So where to catch the bus? And how much is the ticket?" He told me not to catch the bus, join him, he would drive me home. Things couldn't be perfect more than that! It was like things came in the nick of time. I was really excited.

Actually, this Malaysia trip was just a decision without thinking when sitting with Song and she said she would go to Malaysia for some days. I was like "Oh yeah? I will join you". No plan, I didn't have intention to do anything over there. Song travelled with her friend so we may not meetup much, maybe just hangout a bit for coffee.

I wanted this time to be easy, maybe I would just buy some things and relax then go home. When Song knew that I would go to Cameron Highland, she didn't want to let it be like that. She also wanted to join.

But, I was a bit worried because Ryan was just my host on Couchsurfing, I even had never met him before. I didn't know how he would think if I brought along Song and her friend. But I still asked him. Surprisingly, he agreed. He said, "I would drive you all to my hometown". Ryan must be the kindest person I had ever met in Malaysia.

Five in the morning, Ryan drove to my hotel, then we together went to Song's hotel to make sure we could make it to the Cameron Highland by nine for Ryan to vote. From Kuala Lumpur to Cameron Highland, it was 210 km, three-hour drive. The road twisted and turned, so tired. In my previous opinion, West North routes in Vietnam were scary already, but here in Cameron Highland, it was worse.

Although the roads were good quality, smooth, but its curves were impossible to be compared. The car kept moving to the left then to the right, really headache. The two girls sitting in back seat, at the beginning, still joined me to joke with Ryan. Later, they were already too exhausted, didn't want to talk any more. I was in front seat keep on chatting with Ryan. He had woken up too early in the morning, I didn't want him to fall asleep while driving. Chatting also helped the way a bit less long.

Cameron in morning was so fresh and cool. Ryan's house was peaceful on a hill. Ryan brought us out for breakfast. Song, her friend and I played around on grass hills which were so green. We did all kind of poses to take photos and laughed so hard like crazy. We made people turn around and who knew if they were wondering "Are they mental?". Ryan called us when he finished his vote. We met at his house. He used a mini-van to drive all of us to a flower farm. Everybody got excited when knowing that we were heading there. We had imagined it would be an endless field of flowers, hidden behind morning dews. But, we didn't know that a scary journey had just begun…

Over mountains over hills

There were countless kinds of flowers on Cameron Highland. Just like Da Lat, Cameron Highland was the leading producer of flowers in Malaysia and exported to nearby countries like Singapore and Indonesia. From a distance, we could see many big greenhouses located on hills covered in white plastic nylon, separated themselves from the grass area. Ryan's brother worked for a very big greenhouse which seemed to be the highest one in the area.

We got one of the most unforgettable experience on the way reaching the greenhouse. The slope was vertically upwards, looked like they were of 45 degrees or even more. We must hold tight to the van otherwise we would fall out of it. We held on to the van so hard that it was too painful. The brother was already familiar to this road, he drove at high speed.

We were so nervous but felt fun and scared at the same time. However, when we got there, the nervousness was gone. The farm was in its harvesting season, fields that stretched beyond the sight were filled up with blooming flowers. Harvested flowers were gathered in piles. They were all kinds of flowers: daisy, lys, and more. They were fully blooming. The cold air on the highland made everybody feel really fresh. It was not a scene that every traveler was able to observe. Unintentionally, Song and I looked each other and felt truly grateful for this once-in-a-lifetime opportunity.

If it scared the hell out of us on the way up to the farm, it was worse on the way down. We were too nervous that the van may plunge into abyss. The speed plus the steep hill together turned our stomachs upside down. Faces turned into green but impossible to complain. Oh gosh, what an experience!

In the afternoon, another friend of Ryan, named Henry, drove a 7-seated car to bring us around. There were many high hills in Cameron highland. The car was like sneaking into each tea plantations and flower fields. I was strongly impressed by tea plantation business here, it was big and in really good organization, I could see. Cameron Highland was famous for its tea business.

We dropped by the biggest tea house to enjoy a cup of milk tea. The place was designed to be protruding from the mountain, below were greenish tea fields. What a dreamy landscape. I thought I could spend the whole day just to sit there, in this picturesque scene, enjoy the tea freshly plucked from the fields below. When smoke from steamy tea cup mixed with the highland coldness, it would be awesome…

That was the best milk tea I have ever had. It tasted like Phuc Long milk tea[1] but much richer. I even thought I wanted to bring this kind of tea back to Vietnam and do business. Not too bad.

---

1   *Phuc Long Coffee and tea, a tea brand in Vietnamese, famous among young people*

Peaceful Highland

Ryan and Henry drove us passing tea plantations, huge flower fields, ripen juicy strawberry gardens, and green cabbage patches. Being locals, these two friends knew this place thoroughly. They loved it, honored it and passionately introduced it to us – strangers. The two were funny, the whole car were noisy with laughter.

There was a fun story while in strawberry garden. I heard someone call me. I was looking around looking for the caller when I saw Van. I met Van one time only while in Bangkok. Yet maybe God brought us together, in another country – Cameron Highland in Malaysia – I met her again. The world is small, I guessed. Then after that, when we were going to the parking place to get the car, one car stopped by us, there were knock-knock from the inside, the window was rolled down. I turned my head thinking it must be Van saying goodbye. But no, inside the car was another girl. I was a bit confused, then the girl smiled shiningly and said "Em cũng là người Việt Nam nè" (I am Vietnamese, too). How cute it was! Vietnamese saying hello while abroad without even knowing each other…

That evening, Henry wanted Hot Pot for dinner. He said there was a very good place for hot pot, in the neighbor village. We were too tired and hungry already. It was also cold at night. Nothing would serve better than a steamy hot pot. Everybody therefore was so eager to get to the place. Henry drove, but he kept driving and driving.

He always said, "We are almost there, we are almost there" but it looked like we had already finished many hills, and the car just kept going in the darkness. There was no sign of lights or any town/ village. Song was so hungry that she could faint any time, so, without any energy left, she stopped asking. "Wherever you want, I don't care". I threated Henry "If I die of hunger in your car, I would haunt you, man". Contrary to us, Henry still kept calm, and he reassured "Almost there".

We did get there. And Henry didn't lie to us, the hot pot was really delicious. The good smell together with spicy taste in the middle of a quiet cold night among friends, all made me so happy. Ryan and Henry, they were still strangers this morning, now they were like my close friends.

Young people, when they meet each other and share the same mindset, it would not be hard for them to find their mutual similarities and get along with each other. It's like an obvious fact. At night when it was a bit chilly, sitting at a Starbucks, listening to the sounds of English, Chinese, Malaysian and felt like being in a suburb of a European city. Song said, "I thought I were in England?". I myself thought I must have been in Switzerland. It was really the same. It gave me the exact feeling like what I felt when I was in Damiano's small village when we rode to Lugano at night for a mojito. I really love this place, a little peace for my little heart...

THE GULF OF THAILAND: 1,645 KM BY BUS

———

After signing up to host travellers on Couchsurfing.com, I welcomed many interesting friends from all over the world. The first one who couched at my place was a twenty-year-old guy named Chris. Chris was Canadian and travelling around the world. He had been on his trip for two years by the time we met. After Chris was Jia Hao, a Shanghai guy who spoke glish like a native and had covered almost all of Asia. Then a Korean-Australian young man, then Reuben from Puerto Rico, Damiano from Switzerland, and Fumi and Ryan from Malaysia. I kept asking how these guys could be so cool – they worked, they saved money and they set off. I worked too, but then I'd slink into some corner of Saigon and dream about visiting cities without actually going anywhere. I thought I had to put my plan into action one day. People spend money, so they can travel here and there, from West to East. Me? In just six hours I could be in another city where people spoke a different language. So why not? That was how I started.

There is a common feature among my foreign friends: they do not usually have a detailed plan: hotel bookings, destination checklists, what to eat, who to meet, etc. To them, everything is serendipity, every experience would bring meaning to life. They like to experience and above all, they adapt themselves to places.

In contrast, I was worried about many things. With previous trips, I had plans as detailed as the timetable of a primary student: What I would eat in morning, where I would go, what I would do in the afternoon, where I would drink in the evening, which bus to take, which area to stay in, blah blah blah. All of these were because of anxiety. Anxiety results in fear; fear of everything under the open sky. Therefore, this time in the Gulf of Thailand, I wanted a change. No preparation – nothing! This was the first trip I would take with this mindset.

Before I left, I just did some simple things: I made a call to book a bus ticket for Ha Tien and an air ticket from Bangkok to Saigon. Reuben said Otres was the most beautiful beach in Sihanoukville, so okay, fine, that would be the destination, let's go.

Of course, I am no longer that blind now, I absolutely could give you an almost perfect guide, clear and complete… So, shall we start?

CHAPTER 3

CAMBODIA

I had fallen in love with this place already. Not because of something big, not by words-with-wings on travelling websites, and not just to be a copycat. I went to Otres and enjoyed a very simple, very primordial pleasure.

SIHANOUKVILLE A
HEAVEN ON EARTH

Tough start

Exhausted, I went home and hastily packed my things, then got on a sleeping bus after a long day at work. As a result, I forgot my passport. So, you may be thinking, am I another Nobita? Well, it's undeniable; I really am that forgetful. I would not have been able to make it even if someone had brought me the passport since the bus was leaving at 9:00 pm. In the worst scenario, I could get off in Ha Tien, ship off to Phu Quoc and spend some days swimming before heading home. Not too bad…take life as it is, I thought. Then the driver told me there was another bus leaving an hour later, at 10:00 pm, and my passport could be sent with that bus if I waited for it in Ha Tien. Adversity brings luck – every problem has its own solution. The key is that we should cool down and find the solution – not frantically dash this way then that way – there's no need to mess it up.

The story turned out to be interesting. I arrived in Ha Tien at 5:30 am, had a leisurely breakfast and coffee while looking at bustling passers-by. At 6:40 am my passport arrived, and I took a motorbike taxi to Xa Xia border gate. It was some 4 or 5 km from the bus station to the border, I closed a bargain of fifty thousand dong with an old driver who had kind smile to get there. The gate opened at 6:00 am and the immigration process got underway quickly.

(By the way, please note that you should not attach any money to your passport – just go straightforwardly through the whole process. I saw some people did such cringeworthy things. How can we get better as a society if we continue paying bribes?)

Crossing Milepost 313 between the two countries, I left Vietnam behind. Ha Tien Vegas Casino came into view. I was unimpressed. But, compared to the poor surroundings at the border of the two lowdeveloped countries, it seemed massive. My esteemed driver dropped me at the border on the Cambodian side where there were some buses waiting for passengers to go deeper into Cambodia. Some backpackers on Phuot.vn taking the same route via Xa Xia– Sihanoukville said a bus ticket was about 200,000 – 250,000 dong and some paid 300,000 dong. I thought I would copy Westerners and walk around checking to see if I was lucky enough to get a good deal. I seemed to be the only Vietnamese backpacker. At that time, about five years ago, this route was still empty, not crowded like today. After a time of hard bargaining, I found myself on an express bus after an amazing deal: three dollars, or 60,000 dong, for the 160 km journey to the sea. The bus had only two rows for passengers. All the rest were removed to make room for cargo.

At that price, I was quite concerned if the bus would take me to where I needed to be. Would I be kicked out of the bus halfway? Or perhaps their destination was not what I had negotiated? I asked the young boy who was the driver's helper:

"Sihanoukville? Port?"

He reassured me: "Yes, Port."

Then he gave me a kind smile to make me feel better. But to be honest, nobody could make a guy feel better who was on an unknown road leading to a foreign land, and who was on a bus full of weirdsmelling salted fish or whatever it was.

Later, I learnt that there is one port in Cambodia only, which is Sihanoukville. The bus shambled past dusty road construction, high mountains, long peaceful rivers and shabby people in the provincial towns of Kep and Kampot. At 10:30 am, I arrived in Sihanoukville. That meant it had been three-and-a-half hours on the bus. A motorbike driver pulled up:

"Where you go?"

"Otres." I replied quickly

"Three dollars." He offered

"Too much. Just a short run from here." I complained. "One dollar I go."

But I was bargaining without knowing what I was doing since I had never been there. Afterward, I figured out that Otres really was quite far and I felt ruthless to have bargained so hard about this. The motodop reluctantly accepted my offer as he could not win over me. The bike ran on and on, passing towns, grasslands, slopes and... whew... still hadn't arrived yet! Sometimes, there were even white cows flooding over the road and no sign of a beach. Was I getting worried? Well…

Finally, I could hear the sounds of waves and taste salt in the wind. I mentally measured and guessed it was eight kilometers to the sea. I told the driver to bring me to a cheap backpacker's hostel or hotel. He drove me to a hostel on Otres beach whose rate was twelve dollars per person, per night. No way, haha! I made an offer of ten dollars. The receptionist did not agree and then slipped away like a cat. Okay, fine. (Note: saving money was not necessarily the point of every bargain, but rather seeing how well I could adapt and test my skills.)

The driver asked me, "So how much you can pay for a night?" I said, "Ten dollars."

He said OK and took me to another bungalow right on the beach called Tuk-tuk Guesthouse. I walked in and the owner said, Ten dollars.

"Nope, it should be eight." I told him.

"Eight is too cheap. Impossible." The owner replied.

I asked him, "Do you think you wanted too much? Because next week I will have four friends coming…really! You should give me a good price, so then you will have more guests."

And that was how I convinced him and brought in my backpack. I did not forget to pay the driver $1.50 (50% was not a bad tip!)

My bungalow was just ten meters from the sea. And oh, my gosh…

Otres – A heaven on earth

The sea was just within my reach – right there, so close, were handsome boys and cute girls playing in the waves. This was not just a beach, but Heaven with incomparably vast space and water as greenish-blue as turquoise. People were comfortably lounging about under the sunshine. I had been to many beautiful beaches and had previously reached the conclusion that, no matter how beautiful one's surroundings may be, there always be unbeautiful people on the beach. And yet! Here, on this beach, not a single "Unbeautiful" person! I will explain my reasoning later, but here was something I had to accept: I was the worst-looking one on the beach.

The beach was nestled in a bay; therefore, the waves were not big and strong but tiny and gentle. Being the farthest beach in Sihanoukville, Otres was not affected by noisy traffic or a bustling crowd. Of all of the beaches, Otres was the most untouched. Therefore, older visitors would not come here but stayed at beaches that were closer to town. Only idle couples and young people would come all the way out here. So, there was no need to look around to search, for right there, within your sight, were sun-bathing girls in small bikinis, guys with six-packs running for health (or for whatever), couples tenderly applying suncream onto each other (so envious! >_ <), some lazily reading, some even topless…

OK, enough of watching people, back to my own business. I chose for myself a hut which was one meter away from the water and took out my gadgets: book and phone (for Facebook and music), towel, and coke. I asked for a menu to find something to fill my stomach. The waiter gave me a menu with images of ocean stuff – crabs and fishes and shrimp. I ordered a seafood BBQ which cost $4.50 (classy!). So, food: check! Now what? A whole heaven was right there...so tempting it was that I was unable to hold back the desire to join in. C'mon, I was at a beach, right? Let's swim!

So, yes, I did jump down and dive into the turquoise water where I swam in all styles like a boss!

The dust from the morning's journey was swept away. After swimming for quite a time, I relaxed and posted some photos to Facebook. A great smell from the kitchen came to my notice and then I saw the waiter with a huge dish on which were vegetables and grilled seafood – five squids, seven shrimps, and one fish. The seafood here was so fresh. Until then I hadn't really been much into seafood, but that day I realized maybe it was because what I had eaten before was just frozen and tasteless. This time it was really, really good.

All I did the whole day was eating, swimming, and then going back on the beach to sunbathe and read. When I got tired I'd sleep, have a meal after sleeping and then some Coke and then take photos and then swim then... whew... the loop repeated until late afternoon. I loved every minute of it; I don't care how stupid I sound. I do not like to work like a dog...when you're in Heaven, live like you're in Heaven!

In the evening, I rented a motorbike to ride around the town and other beaches. Sihanoukville was beautiful and untouched (pfff, hardly!). People here were kind and friendly. I took lots of photos for Facebook – endless meadows, lazy white cows grazing under the burning sunshine, calm lakes reflecting lonely trees, wild monkeys running freely on forest through-roads, beaches with water as clear as crystal... My friends really liked my photos.

The ocean during sunset was a beautiful work of art when the sun reddened like a fire ball and sank under a blanket of turquoise. I was shirtless, lying motionless on the beach in such a state of tranquility that the sound of the waves lulled me into the belief that time might be standing still. Right here, right now; no more reports, no more living paycheck-to-paycheck, no other passions, no more mediocre desires, no more big dreams, no more struggling love, nothing... Only the purest and calmest thoughts, thoughts which gave me peace. I realized that I should strive to live simply; as simply as the exquisite moment I watched the sun creep down, little by little, into darkness. You and I – all of us – will one day lie down and give in to the darkness, just like that.

I had fallen in love with this place already. Not because of something big, not by words-with-wings on travelling websites, and not just to be a copycat. I went to Otres and enjoyed a very simple, very primordial pleasure. Many foreigners chose Sihanoukville to be their stop for life. I saw many Westerners along the way riding motorbikes to local markets. They gave me directions like locals when I asked them.

And it turned out, after a short chat, they had come for a couple of years and had no intention of leaving...

My Otres in daylight was that shimmering, that beautiful, that dreamy. But when darkness took over, I could not help the long yawn. "What I am going to do now?"

Break the darkness

Night in Otres was torture for solo travellers and partypeople. After the sun had completely sunk into the silver, glimmering water, there was left an atmosphere of terrible silence. It wasn't the vibrant and bustling coastal tourist place one came to expect from such destinations. No, things here were completely different.

Lights were quite dim, waves were lapping, insects were humming, and mosquitoes were helicopters hovering overhead. A big question popped up in my head: would I be able to lie here all night? I itched for the hectic life out there. I wanted to have a cup of coffee! I wanted to grab a cold beer in a pub! But what should I do now?

A brilliant idea flashed through my mind: ride to other beaches. I decided to act upon what I had thought. I may not be good at much, but I can make decision quickly and efficiently! Thinking too much about it is just wasting time and ages us faster.

I sped out of Otres on my scooter. Everything was completely dark. Even at the junction where there were some makeshift family homes, the smoulder of oil lamps made it look like Vietnam from decades ago. I drove slowly passing those rundown shelters, partly because the road was dusty, and partly because I was nervous about running into some kids playing in the middle of the road. But what scared me the most was the stares of small groups of people training their eyes on passers-by. But really – the spook was just my own feeling, everything was actually dark and black, only the occasional head appearing from rugged houses were ever visible.

After passing that five-hundred-meter block, I grew concerned. Imagine this: a completely dark road, with neither a single human nor light nor bike; a road with many potholes and garishly red dust. On both sides of the road were earth mounds, bushes and big ponds, and only the sound of insects humming. In particular, it was very cold. On that road, there was one person only – me – riding a tiny scooter gripped by the darkness. I had read enough bad news and ghost stories from Cambodia and Thailand that they now made me shiver at the sight of even my own shadow. Previously, while travelling, I did have some fears but those were the fears of humans. While at this moment, I feared ghosts.

In this inhospitable jungle and mountain terrain, who knows what could happen? Therefore, after five hundred meters of riding in darkness, I shuddered and decided to turn back.

Back at Tuk-tuk guesthouse, I still felt a lingering longing. I shouldn't waste a night like this, right? Time was limited but the road was still long ahead. In addition, I reasoned, I had already had a slow and peaceful afternoon, so I wanted a vibrant and delightful evening. I approached the guesthouse's owner who was cooking under the poor light:

"I want to go to the town, is it safe?" I asked.

"I'm not sure, but I have never heard of any murders here," He answered.

"Oh gosh, I am scared of the word "murder", even if you had said NO to my question, it still scares me!"

"Ha ha, don't go if you are scared. But I think it should be ok…"

I found and decided to cling to my only defense: I look Cambodian, with t-shirt and shorts, riding solo. They would guess that I was local and would not do anything harmful! That thinking worked like a charm. I gathered my confidence and sped down the road for eight kilometers.

The darkness again swallowed me as the cold wind whipped into my face just like before. Whenever I saw a light, I felt as excited as seeing mom coming home from the market. But the fear kept rising up inside my head. I was scared of everything. Passing the junction, over the bridge, over some ramps and bushes, I found myself there with civilization. I tried not to think about the fact that the road back at midnight would be even more horrible. But then another thought: "If the darkness scares me enough, then I'll just party overnight and go back when it's morning already haha".

I arrived at Occheuteal beach which was full of tourists. At night, there were still girls in bikinis walking around. Where the hell was this where everybody was wearing hardly anything – so cool! This beach was connected to the town, so it was busy and bustling, like the beach in Nha Trang or Vung Tau[2]. In my excitement of discovery, I rode everywhere and all the way to the tiled walking road on the beach. And what a road! Too many people – hard for vehicles. Finally, I reached the end of the road, at which point I asked a vendor:

---

2   *Nha Trang and Vung Tau are two popular beaches in Vietnam*

"Hey, why does the road stop here? How do I go further?" "How did you get here?" He asked surprisedly.

"I just followed the road. What's up?" I answered.

"Because this is a pedestrian path. You are violating the law. You will get fined if the police find you!"

"What the...?"

No wonder I hadn't seen any scooters on this "road" while everybody kept staring at me. I thought I was just handsome. The truth: I was in trouble.

"So how do I get out of here?" I asked him.

"Take my back door, you will see a path. Follow it." He kindly showed me the way out.

I kept thanking him and quickly revved to the back of the place, following the path out to the big road. By the time I got out there, a police van had arrived to go on patrol. How lucky I was!

Like all the previous solo backpacking trips, I chose a Western bar where there were outdoor chairs and ordered a cold beer. There I watched passers-by, observed the nightlife, and chatted with some people. Then I went home.

With a bit of alcohol, I felt better. The way back was shorter. The fear was lesser. And the need for speed was more. The scooter vroomed at full capacity, and it sounded like somebody was following me from behind... Whatever, I feared nothing now!

I returned to my quiet place – Otres – which was already deep in its sleep and had become a bit depressing. I went around the beach in the dim light, lay down on a bench close to the water listening to the waves and hummed "Ước gì em ở đây giờ này…" (Wishing you were here…). Unintentionally, this atmosphere made people way too cheesy. The feeling of "just me, myself and I" among this immense backdrop felt like someone had taken all of my breath away. The waves lapped gently, and I was with my gentle, innermost feelings…

It rained in Otres at midnight. In a light sleep alone in a bungalow near the water, I heard the sound of lapping waves, the patter of the rain onto the cottage roof and sounds of nigh, which all gently kept me awake. Have you ever heard the song "Biển vắng" (Lonely beach) by Ngoc Lan? I've listened to it many times and I've called it my favorite. But that night, I completely felt it. Silent as grave, no human noise, no life sounds… Only the drip-drops of rain and the pound-crash of waves. It was empty and lonely, like I was aging for one hundred years.

The morning after the night rain was gloomy and quiet. I intended to wake up early for the sunrise. In Vietnam, you cannot just go to the beach and sleep late in morning – watching the sunrise is a must. But then I realized the sunrise couldn't be seen over the ocean in Sihanoukville because the beaches here are to the West! No one wakes up early for that! (Well, maybe just me, a guy from Vietnam?) Morning on beach was too quiet with only the sound of waves talking to the wet sand after the rain last night. I could even hear the sound of distant fishermen casting their nets. Far in the distance were islands and motionless boats enveloped in the grey morning landscape…

LOST IN ANGKOR

———

I believe we don't need much money to satisfy our wanderlust desire. I travel to open wide my arms and embrace new things, not only to travel, not only to discover, and not even for spiritual purpose. But when those purposes are combined – a little of this a little of that – so that it's not too much, that's the essence of why I travel.

To travel does not require something luxurious – it can be something simple like the feeling of standing alone in any foreign place. If you have more money, you can go farther. But if not, you are still able to have wonderful days of wandering in Angkor with thousands-year-old heritage. Angkor does not fail to live up to its name to be "a must-see in life". It takes about twelve hours by bus to travel from Sai Gon to this forgotten town.

It felt really overwhelming when I arrived. I love cultural and historical stuff which record the movement of time in a very special and charming way. Here, such recordings were everywhere. Stone statues, walls, and temples lay there, exposing themselves to time. If we invest enough to seek out information about them, we would understand how great they are. How could those huge stones be transported up to the highest tips of the temples? How can those Buddha be smiling? How can my mind keep asking those questions?

Every single time I was there, I lost myself in those ancient mazes of temples which hid themselves in thick layers of forests. I can't take my eyes off of small temples when passing by an unnamed one. These small ones were not introduced to people by tour guides.

The initial plan was to rent a bike or motorbike and drive around to discover it myself, but after looking at the map, I knew it was not a wise thing to do. The whole park was wide and expansive. If I did it myself, I would not be able to get to many places. Not to mention the everpresent sunshine in this country which discouraged me. It was best to hire a tuk-tuk, so that not only I could have a little bit of shadow, but also I could meet other people and get more information about the place. It surprised me that the tuk-tuk driver could speak such good English.

A strange thing was that when I visited the biggest three temples – Angkor Thom, Angkor Wat and Bayon, it was initially fresh and cool on the way. However, by the time I arrived there, it was raining. It started as just a light shower and then it became heavier. That day it rained three times and coincidently all three were at the moments I stepped into temples. Weird, right? And a bit creepy. I hoisted my camera and took photos of every mossy corner, shot whatever came before my eyes, from the outside, to the inside. There were places where it was completely empty, no one but me, places where there was no light, just darkness and the sound of rain falling constantly on the roof of the temple... I suddenly felt scared. A fear that pressed my mind, but excited at the same time. I just stepped forward and knew nothing waited for me ahead. Did I ever worry I would get lost? Of course, I did. But it didn't stop me. And how strange that by the time I stepped out of the temples, it had stopped raining. I kept moving…

When darkness fell, I took a tuk-tuk to the night market and walked around the backpackers' area which was festive and busy. Night in this strange city was nothing fun, nothing sad, nothing to think about. It was just people passing by in colors, all races, under the yellowful light of the night in Angkor. I liked this feeling: alone, no interaction, my eyes aptly recorded all things happening around. Then I entered Temple Bar.

The music was so loud that I had to use gestures to let the waiter know that I needed a table for one and ordered a tequila; a drink so strong that you could feel where it was into your body. The tequila warmed me up. I spent the whole night sitting there just to look, and watch people dancing and drinking… One shot cost two dollars – not too expensive – and we could have as many as we wanted, but it made my head hot and achey; even more intensely because of the loud music. I decided to stop after my second drink. Getting drunk is not a wise thing to do at night when travelling alone…

I took the same way back to my hostel, passed by a street vendor and stopped for a dish of fried rice with vegetables. The lady asked: "Vietnam?" and I replied affirmatively, then sat down for a leisurely meal. My default speed is fast – eating fast, speaking fast, sleeping fast – everything must be fast. But it is said that people who always rush have hard life, they are always busy, worried, and can't rest like people who take it slow and easy. In moments like these I thought about this and prefered to be slow and easy; to calm down, to feel my surroundings become clearer... I got lost on the way, even when I knew to where it led...

I usually think illustratively that life is like a white canvas, and no one but I can sit down and paint my own life. If I don't make it an interesting painting, then what will it look like?

Before leaving Angkor to continue this trip, I thought about how crazy my life had been; so many things around me had happened that they jumbled together in a crazy mess in my mind. Therefore, while in Angkor, I stepped into the main shrine, burned a stick of incense and prayed. I prayed for many, many things, and then left a onedollar note. One dollar was hardly enough for so many wishes, but I was determined that this would not be the end of my journey. If my plans came true, I would return on my knees and give thanks for fate's protection and generosity.

By the time my bus reached Sai Gon after the trip, I had the feelings that the universe was telling me "Everything is fine already." Was it magic? Thank the Buddha...

CHAPTER 4

———

THAILAND

And when passing by Buddha in the center of Siam, I initially couldn't help feeling surprised when I saw young boys and girls in fashionable outfits, holding LV bags, on their knees, respectfully offering a prayer and then continuing on their ways. I thought when society developed, traditional values would break down. But the moment I saw that scene, I realized that now, more than ever, is a time when traditional values need to be honored and preserved.

KOH CHANG

———

Across the Gulf of Thailand

I decided to continue my trip to Koh Chang. To get to Koh Chang, I had to travel along the Gulf of Thailand from Sihanoukville, reach Koh Kong, which is in the border with Thailand, then cross the border at Hat Lek to Trat province. After that, I caught a ferry to Koh Chang. Altogether, it was a journey of more than ten hours. However, I didn't mind because I was looking forward to meeting a friend there.

I left Tuk-Tuk guesthouse and went into the town by tuk-tuk to find a bus. It was only $25 USD to go to Koh Chang by bus and ferry. I looked around, and noticed most passengers were foreigners, so I thought it would be safe and felt secure… maybe the service would not be too bad. The bus started off, and we traveled through open forest areas, across wide rivers, around big lakes, through small villages, and dry fields.

Knowing it was a long way, I brought along a big book: Tiny Times by Guo Jing Ming. I did not know why but I liked Shanghai and that was why I wanted to read it. It was actually a good book and helped me get through the lengthy trip of a dozen hours. The whole time I just read, slept and read then looked out at the landscape and read some more. At about three in the afternoon, we reached Koh Kong. People got off the bus. There were only a few people left – me and about six other foreigners. We kept on going to the Hat Lek border-gate which was on the sea. I could hear the sound of the ocean while standing at the immigration counter. Just one more step to the other side… It felt like Cambodia had been behind the times for decades. And then I ran into what I could later learn was a typical border scam:

While standing in the queue for the exit procedure, a Cambodian middleman saw my green passport and approached to ask if I was from Vietnam.

"Uh" I started to reply.

He cut in and told me that Vietnamese people may not be allowed to get through. Vietnamese must bring their passport to the Thai side and check if they would be allowed to cross, and if so, then they could return and do the exit procedure in Cambodia. I did not show any interest and said "thanks", then stayed in my line. He pressed on to say if I did not believe him, I could ask the two Vietnamese over there who were doing same. I looked over and heard them speaking Vietnamese. I played it cool but what the middleman had said actually made me anxious. It would be disappointing if I came all this way only to be rejected by immigration – which looked possible because I didn't look like I had much clout travelling alone with only a backpack. Moreover, since there were two other

Vietnamese seemingly following his directions, maybe it would be a good idea to comply… The guy kept offering "Help" but he couldn't speak English very well, so I decided to ask those two Vietnamese for clarification. The two guys explained the middleman would bring my passport to the Thai border for a precheck – for a fee, of course. Well, better safe than sorry, I supposed. I gave my passport to the dirty Cambodian middleman. After a while, he returned said it was fine and I begrudgingly gave him five dollars.

After finishing the check-out process. I walked to the check-in counter on the Thai side. I have to say that I was becoming nervous by this point because I was the last passenger from our group. The others had already finished their crossing and their luggage was already loaded onto the next bus. If something went wrong at this point, I would be screwed. So, this time when I got to the other side, I did not have a middleman do anything; I did it all myself: filled in the arrival card, put three dollars into my passport and gave it to the immigration officer. He opened my passport, took the money and gave it back to me while smiling kindly and nodded his head. Stamped! Done! This time I got through it – without paying a bribe. While leaving the counter, I saw the two Vietnamese guys busy reading information for their middleman to fill in the immigration card. Ok, I noted triumphantly, they were wasting another amount of money for sure.

What annoyed me was the style of Vietnamese – we think of offering bribes everywhere. That kind of "culture" matches perfectly with Cambodian values. I recalled the haughty, know-it-all attitude of the two Vietnamese I met at the border and felt indignant. What if Vietnamese travellers don't have money to bribe? It's because we don't know the process and don't speak fluent English that make us vulnerable to doing those things. I lost five dollars for being gullible. But it's okay. I just took it as a lesson; something I could share with my friends later and warn them to avoid such scams. Just accept it and continue on without worry.

Everything was completely different on the other side of the border. The bus was better. The roads were better, too. However, in contrast to the friendliness of the scene and its people, we encountered tough check-points with armed policemen armed policemen walking around. We were stopped at every check-point along the way. I was not sure how the police chose their targets – two other Asians who looked like they might have been Cambodian were the only ones singled out for checking. The Westerners and I were not. But I was still worried.

The bus went through a downpour in the middle of an open forest and it made things feel even gloomier. Time seemed to stand still in the midst of the forest rain. By the time the bus pulled in to the station, everybody was exhausted. I dragged my backpack along and showed my Koh Chang ticket. Then I got on a vehicle which resembled a tuktuk which transported me to the ferry for the island. On the ferry were only me, a French couple, an old Israeli man and an American couple. After a long trip, everybody was tired but the fact that we were going to the island made us more cheerful. I managed to ask them to help me take some photos for memory. And I also began to cheer up as I anticipated meeting my close friend from Vietnam who had been there before and was waiting for me.

Message on the desert island

I arrived Koh Chang at nearly eight in the evening. The bus stopped on the main road near its night market. The market was quite…poor, incomparable to the bustling ones in places like Pattaya, Phuket Chiang Mai, or Krabi.

Koh Chang, a.k.a. Chang Island or Elephant Island, is the second biggest island in Thailand of Trat Province in the east. The island is a part of the Mu Koh Chang National Park, 310 km away from Bangkok. Elephant Island gets its name because it has an elephant shape – elephants are not indigenous to the island. There are eight villages on the island and many waterfalls and high mountains too, the highest one at 744 m. Koh Chang's total land area is about 429 km square and is surrounded by 51 smaller islands. (Wiki)

Armed with some vague information collected from the internet, I actually knew little about this place, but that was actually done on purpose – I didn't want to be distracted or persuaded by the feelings of people who had come here before. I wanted to discover and experience it all for myself.

Everyone on my bus had already booked their accommodation, except for the French couple, so I joined them to find a guesthouse. After checking many, we found a small hostel at the foot of a mountain at a very good rate of $15 USD per night. But actually, my priority was not to find a place to sleep, but to have Wi-Fi to check email and Facebook. Unfortunately, this $15 USD guesthouse was too cheap for Wi-Fi, so I bid farewell to the French couple and went around to find a coffee shop, with Wi-Fi.

When I finally found one, I sat down and excitedly open up Facebook…

"I am still in BKK, bro. I can't go to Koh Chang. See you in BKK…"

That was the scariest message I could have received while on the island. My friend wasn't coming which meant, "Tam, enjoy the desert island ALONE!" I was shocked. Our agreement was to meet up and go back to Bangkok together. That was a great plan! Now? Everything was screwed up!

Fine. Keep calm.

I went back to the guesthouse.

The guesthouse was unusual that the surrounding area was so spacious that they built the rooms separate from each other by a space of 10 meters. In that 10-meter-space, there were bushes, insects, and not much light. Oh, my goodness, I was on an island with this kind of guesthouse, was I going to DIE?

I said the guesthouse was $15/night. But actually, I sure wasn't going to agree to that. I told the receptionist I was staying alone – using MUCH less water than the French couple. Needless to say, I am Asian, so there must be a special discount. She smiled and said "Ok, give you special price: $12 USD." And she added "Promise me, don't tell the couple".

Of course, I was not crazy enough to tell them! That three dollars I saved would be used to buy some sleeping pills or cardiac medication. C'mon, staying in this spooky place was like acting in a Thai horror movie.

Koh Chang at night was surprisingly quiet. The main road was too short and pretty dark because of the only one yellow streetlight. Small beer bars squatted along the road with dark old ladies tiredly watching people without bothering to greet them. I walked around to find something to eat, chose a porridge place, ate in a hurry then went for a walk around.

Luckily, there was a coffee shop – the one I had visited previously for Facebook, which was beautiful. Up to this day in my memory, I remember it as the most beautiful coffee shop I have ever seen. It was quite small. There were some stylish tables and chairs outside and the walls were fully glass so that people could see inside. They served kiwi smoothies which were ridiculously delicious. Whenever I think about a coffee shop, that place in Koh Chang is the one which inspires me the most. Unfortunately, I was too exhausted to take a picture of it but it's still deeply embedded in my mind.

The guesthouse at the foot of the mountain

After leaving the transparent coffee shop, I intended to go back to the guesthouse but I didn't feel good about it. Thinking about the isolated room at the foot of a mountain surrounded by insects made me shiver. Usually, I was the one telling my friends scary stories, but at that moment, I felt scared myself.

Ok, so let's find another option.

I dropped by a bar along the beach, watched a fire dance and ordered a mojito. With a bit of alcohol, my face became hot. Maybe it would help me sleep better. Really, I needed a good sleep after the whole day on the bus.

My room was on the most famous beach in Koh Chang, White Sand Beach. What a dear name, huh? I dreamed of white sandy beaches, where beautiful people sunbathed under the blazing sunshine, where I could behave like them, lying on my back with a fresh drink and book in hand. However, the morning I woke up and walked to the beach, I discovered my imagination had been way off, and my mood took a nosedive. The beach was dirty with sand that was black. Where was the famous white sand??? They tricked me! Oh, my goodness, Thais – they did it so well – turning No into Yes.

I've since come to realize that in Thailand, all beaches, be they pretty or ugly, all have beautiful names. Not like in Vietnam where there are ugly names for paradise beaches – Doc Let, Mui Ne, or Sao, Say, Nha Chay (Burnt House), Burnt Grass, blah blah blah… Oh my goodness, they were like beautiful girls with terrible names.

My bad impressions made me unhappy to be here. If I was not happy to be here, I reasoned, I should move on. So I reduced my unhappiness with an early goodbye, I packed my backpack to leave Koh Chang with a deep disappointment that I couldn't meet my friend and had to stay in a scary guesthouse by a mountain listening to cats meowing in the middle of the night which sounded like a crying baby.

I left for Bangkok. After checking out Couchsurfing.com, an Indian guy agreed to host me in Bangkok. Actually, I had wanted to stay with a Thai person to better understand local life, but I couldn't find a Thai host on time. That's ok – staying with an Indian would be a new experience and would still serve my purpose of saving a night in a hotel.

Now let's go to Bangkok.

BANGKOK

———

Avneesh Kabra

Bangkok welcomed me with a heavy night rain, Bangkok – the city was not flashy as usual but gloomy. After eight hours on the bus, I needed a place to shower and lie down. The bus station was in Khao San, the area where if it hadn't been raining, would have been festive. Backpackers were sitting in local beer places sadly looking at the rain – maybe they were estimating when it would stop so they could get wasted. I rushed into a 7Eleven, bought a SIM card to call my Indian host and the friend I was supposed to meet on Koh Chang. The Indian streamed out directions for how to get to his place in a bunch of gluey English (like Indians do!), and my friend said he would meet me in the Pat Pong night market for a beer later. Now, I headed to the Indian's place, ready to hang out.

My host was an Indian named Avneesh Kabra. He was very considerate. Avneesh had been to Vietnam once and particularly loved Vietnamese. Therefore, when he saw my request for a host on Couchsurfing, he agreed without any hesitation.

Avneesh waited for me at home to give me the basics about stuff like keys, how to get around, how to use the cooker, Wi-Fi password, etc. Avneesh and his two other Indian housemates had come here to work for a software company and rented a three-bedroom apartment. His place was right there in the center, just a five-minute walk to Asok Skytrain station. From there, I could go to anywhere in the city.

I had been to Bangkok a couple of times before, so I had only tepid excitement for this city. However, Avneesh's care made me really happy to be there. He brought me around to different places and I followed without telling him I had already been to those places and actually knew them pretty well. I did not want to dampen his excitement. And anyway, I had no other plans except to spend time with him; let him be my guide and absorb his excitement. Bangkok by night was shining – people from all over the world come here to party, to laugh, and to have fun.

Prior to this experience I did not have a good impression of Indians simply because in banking, Indians were usually dictatorial, worked tirelessly and could be very annoying. However, meeting Avneesh changed my impression by making me learn that there were kind and nice Indians. Actually, there are many kinds of people everywhere. It's just luck or not that we meet the good or bad ones.

On the day of my leaving, Avneesh drove me to the Skytrain, shook my hand and waited until I disappeared from his sight. I received an email later:

"Thanks for the great reference, though I'm not sure if I deserve it. Either way, next time you come to Bangkok, I'll definitely make time to hang out with you.

Take care and have fun.

Cheers!"

And how about my friend, the deserter? My friend had a girlfriend and he told me the reason he couldn't go to Koh Chang was because his girlfriend had something suddenly come up during the time. The beauty killed the knight. Although I was still pissed off, I excused him by making him pay for the beer.

I returned to Sai Gon and resumed my busy days: rushing to work in mornings, hustling among colleagues for lunches at noon, going to the usual coffee places in the evenings. But in my dreams, I was floating on long buses, having my ears softened by the sound of waves along the Gulf of Thailand. 1645 km across the gulf but they were still there in my mind. Why not?

A girl with two faces

It is said that Bangkok is a two-faced girl.

To tourists coming in on a tour, Bangkok is a bad girl, debauched and playful. Tourists go to lively sex shows, to streets flooded with flowers and lights, to cool areas where they get lost in fun. Tours are designed to be very tight: bus – eat – bus – play – bus – shopping – bus – eat – bus – play – etc. All they say when they go home is: "Oh

Bangkok is full of transgenders who are as beautiful as princess", "OMG, what a country – full of sex!", "Oh it's so free over there", and then, "Okay, it's time, get on the bus or you stay here – we don't wait."

The buses are always ready to go, they the tourists just need to get on. It's not the fault of tour agencies, it is just to be safe. Tour guides repeat the same old information about people and country and I am pretty sure that those who come to Bangkok learn nothing at all about it. It's like you go to a show of things which are outstanding and flashy, but you forget that there are still hidden corners which are simple, familiar and non-touristy.

But Bangkok is not only parties and flash. This is just a small part of Thai culture. Local Thais do not go to those places, they consider that to be their shame. It's only tourists who go there every night, wanting more and more... And how maddening it is when people who've never visited Bangkok put a label on those who travel there and say, "Oh, they just go there for sex and fun." How narrowed-minded!

There is the other face of the girl, of Bangkok: sincere, authentic, real and charming. Take, for example, the 7Eleven stores that are at every corner of Bangkok. How lovely it is when we get exhausted at 1:00 am and enter the store to buy a cup of instant noodles, and slurp it while walking back to hotel. And milk (milk is quite tasty in Thailand), or energy drinks for walking days and variety of candy, etc. All that we need is right there in that small corner store. And my favorited part is when the cashiers say the amount in Thai. Hey cutie, I don't understand, but I enjoy the look of confusion on your face and I love your shy smile when I ask, "How much?" in English.

I liked the BTS the most and I used it a lot. Motorbike taxis and the MRT were my second choices. I usually stood against the walls, wore headphones, and got off quickly when I reached my station just like a local. I am pretty sure people who travel with a tour don't know anything about the BTS or the MRT (Well, if they have never been to a developed country, that is). I figured out where I wanted to go, bought tickets, decided on the direction, got on the train and daydreamed while looking out of the windows when the train passed by high-rise buildings. I even enjoyed standing in the queue to get on the trains! It's civilized with no pushing or bumping into others. How modern I was!

I also enjoyed strolling around until I was exhausted and then dropped by a fast massage place, rewarded myself with a dim sleep while stretching my muscles and recovering my energy. Or dropping into a Starbucks to have a drink – any drink that could refresh my aching throat – or stumbling onto a street vendor with a vegetable buffet which was so cheap. And when they learnt that I was a traveler, I enjoyed seeing their surprised faces because "No tourists come to this area".

But just like everybody else, I agree that the shopping malls in Bangkok cannot be missed – good stuff is abundant at cheaper prices than in my home country. I particularly like clothes by brands like H&M, Zara, and G2000 where one can buy shirts, trousers, shoes, belts, underwear, etc. with the best prices. I take trips to Bangkok annually just to buy clothes from those brands. Or it can take your breath away when you are in higher-end shops like Bossini, Giordano, Body Glove, or Top man. For women: Mango, Topshop or Berkha. I often stroll around Robinson where, oh my gosh, there are usually massive sales. Luckily, most of the clothes on sale are bigger than my size, so I don't drop too much money on anything! But jeans, shoes, bags are ok and accessories aren't too bad. Or if you want to find things that are even cheaper, go to Chatuchak Market at the weekend. I guarantee, you'll get lost!

I also love to go to the Wats[3] along the legendary Chao Phraya River. All tours include a visit to these wats but the difference is the tour group never uses the small passenger boats which run along the river. It's only by boat where you can feel the river breeze, can see fish under the water, or ogle big hotels along the two banks of the river. Passengers on boats are all kinds: students, monks, vendors, travellers… thousands of faces with thousands of lives to observe and to reflect upon.

And when passing by Buddha in the center of Siam, I initially couldn't help feeling surprised when I saw young boys and girls in fashionable outfits, holding LV bags, on their knees, respectfully offering a prayer and then continuing on their ways. I thought when society developed, traditional values would break down. But the moment I saw that scene, I realized that now, more than ever, is a time when traditional values need to be honored and preserved.

---

3   Wat: in Thai, it means temple

In my opinion, vanity which comes easily will easily go again. If I could choose only one thing to remember, I would choose something close, something familiar, something simple. It is those aforementioned simple things that make up Bangkok in my heart. I could stay there a whole week, just to wake up late in mornings, walk around finding something to eat, then go buy something, then go to the cinema, then get on the BTS to somewhere, else just like any local.

If Hong Kong and Singapore have already lost their sense of the Orient, or if Cambodia, Laos and Myanmar are still in their dream of the past, Bangkok is a mixed child. It is the intersection of cultures – the Orient and Occident. You must go to feel it, even just once.

AYUTTHAYA

———

Sleeping temples

From Hua Lam Phong railway station, I took the train to Ayutthaya, an ancient town, a Kingdom has been in a deep sleep for centuries – a world heritage site since November 1991.

If someone asks me what's interesting about Thailand, I would say it's not the bustle of Bangkok; neither the non-stop sex tours nor shopping from morning to night, but it's the temples along the Chao Praya River, the beliefs I have never seen, and above all is the place – sacred and mysterious Ayutthaya. Ayutthaya composes a scene which is at once magnificent and antique, immense and strange, serene and peaceful.

My initial motivation to go there was because I was charmed by the photos that Vũ took during his time in Bangkok. Being 76 km away from Bangkok, one can take a bus or train to Ayutthaya. I chose a local train costing only eight thousand Vietnam dongs where I could watch the landscape of windy fields flash before my eyes through wide open windows. In my head, I kept thinking "Oh, the train has reached Phan Thiet or Phan Rang[4]" because the view outside looked so much like those places in my country. Similar except for the typical Thai stilt houses along the way.

A Thai person asked us: "You are from Vietnam?"

Surprised, I asked him: "How do you know?"

He said he had overheard the phrase ăn cơm[5] while we were talking. Just a little thing but made me feel at home – that's how Thai people promote tourism; from the very little things.

I was sitting with a group of three Vietnamese; two people I met on the plane, another I made friends with awhile back on the bus and then myself. I was sorry that my American friend was late and couldn't make it but he asked me to take as many photos as possible. I sat quietly without talking while wearing headphones and sunglasses. Sometimes, I'd take random photos.

I had just joined the group to have some companions but honestly, I didn't want my feelings to be influenced. That is the reason why I usually travel alone to cities. I prefer, at the first taste of a place, that all emotions to be for me only. I may end up liking it or not, but one thing for sure is my genuine feelings; not someone else's.

We arrived close to noon while the sun was shining directly overhead. But nothing can outshine the excitement of discovery. We hired a tuk-tuk and chose where we would visit. I was here – the very place portraited in my mind by Vu's photos. I was here, had

---

4   *Phan Thiet, Phan Rang: central provinces of Vietnam*

5   Ăn cơm (Vietnamese): have meal

my hands on red bricks, the headless Buddha statues, untouched markers of time.

I wanted to cycle all day long in the big park, under century-old trees and shadows of timeless temples and majestic statues.

I was really overwhelmed by wonder of the landscape of this place, so I kept shooting photos. I normally like to be the one who is photographed; but in front of this kind of scene, I wanted to capture everything to avoid having it fade in my memory. The feeling was so overwhelming that it nearly brought tears to my eyes - I felt tiny in a huge and tranquil world.

I climbed high to shoot down the whole scene, I crawled along on my knees to try to capture my admiration and to let my mind travel further. This town was more than I expected. It deserved to be preserved.

We visited many places over noon to ensure we could be back to Bangkok on time. Our shirts were damp with sweat but no one felt tired, because every place had its own looks and artefacts to be remembered so we strove to visit as many as possible.

At the end of the day, we managed to catch the last bus back to Bangkok. It was a crowded bus and as usual I put on my headphones to reflect upon my own thoughts.

I wondered "Am I...kinda brave?" – Carrying a backpack to a foreign country, learning to use their local transport and absorbing everything I experienced. ALONE – Yes. Yes, I think I am. Well, I made it, anyway. Like they said "Just go and you will find a way".

ALONE IN CHIANG MAI

———

New friends

If in Bangkok, it would be a pity not to pay a visit to Chiang Mai. I usually call this city "Hue[6] in Dalat[7]" because of its structure and the weather. Chiang Mai is breathlessly beautiful, and painfully peaceful... Someday, if I ever have to name just one place that I would want to come back to, I would say without hesitation: Chiang Mai.

After visiting Ayutthaya, I travelled back to Bangkok with my close friends. After that my friends flew back to Saigon and I continued my journey.

After seeing my friends off to the airport, I took the BTS back to the stop near my hotel. I trudged along, counting each step and occasionally looking back to confirm that no one was there... everyone had gone home... It was a bit lonely...

———

6   *Huế: a city in central Vietnam that was the seat of Nguyen Dynasty emperors and the national capital from 1802 to 1945. A major attraction is its ruined citadel from 19th century, surrounded by a moat and thick stone walls. It encompasses the Imperial City, with palaces and shrines; the Forbidden Purple City was once the emperor's home.*

7   *Đà Lạt: the capital of Lâm Đồng Province in Vietnam. The city is located 4,900 ft above sea level in the southern parts of the Central Highlands region. Da Lat is a popular tourist destination with year-round cool weather.*

Suddenly, I felt sad, extremely sad. That feeling when the party is over and your house is empty – left with just me, myself and I – was so terrible, like someone had thrown you into a black hole and you fell sank into it without gravity.

As planned, I would check out of the hotel and take a train to Chiang Mai. The last train of the day would be at 10pm. With bags packed, I sprawled out in my hotel room and all of a sudden I didn't want to go anymore, I wanted to change my ticket back to Sai Gon – but that was impossible unless I was willing to pay a huge amount for different airfare rates.

I shouldn't be so lame, right?

I gathered myself, packed up and checked out of the hotel. I left my big wheeled case and brought only my backpack with some clothes to the Hua Lam Phong railway station. It was 9:00 pm, should be fine to catch the last train.

BUT!

Shocking news: Tickets sold out.

It was the end of the year; everybody was going home. Lost!! My mind spun furiously – "What should I do now? Back to the hotel? And then spend four days doing the same old things: Silom night market, foot massage, beer?".

While I was desperately trying to think of a solution, a railway officer came and asked my destination.

"Chiang Mai," I said, "but no more tickets."

"Same here," a pretty white girl standing next to him smiled and said. "So… what are you gonna do?" I asked her.

"Well, I'm going to wait to see if someone cancels their tickets" she said. "You should hang on a bit."

I expected nothing, but still decided to stay and chat. That was fun anyway. I learned she was from Canada. Some minutes later, the officer was back with news.

"Hey, only a third-class left, you want it?"

Honestly, until that point, I had never been on a train. First class or third class, I didn't know the difference. I just wanted to go so I nodded my head and jumped. The Canadian woman and her Norwegian travel companion were not in the same carriage.

From here began the torture – the torture I will never forget, that burns in my memory with such awfulness that it's taken on a sweet legend status…

Third class means sitting… sitting up for 14 hours from Bangkok to Chiang Mai. That doesn't sound too bad, right? Maybe just like sitting on a bus? NO. Life is not a dream so life will kill the dream! As it was getting late, it was getting colder. Chiang Mai is further to the north and mountainous, so the air became horribly cold. I put on my jacket and shoes but still felt freezing. I even covered my face – it didn't help. The coldness felt like daggers everywhere always ready to stab and I couldn't hide from it. I was cold but even worse was I couldn't sleep. I woke up every 15 minutes because it was so cold and cramped.

And because it was a cheap ticket, its passengers were also stuffed together. A whole family talked loudly, a guy in soldier's outfit holding wine scolded me noisily in Thai (I didn't get it, I wouldn't take it!), kids crying, and a student sitting next to me asking perky, half-formed questions, like: "New Year Chiang Mai, huh? Cold, huh? Vietnam, huh? Beautiful! (Oh God!), "White you, me black", blah blah... To sum up, it was tiring. How the hell had I ended up here?

My mood didn't get better through the night. The mist obscured the view making it impossible to see anything out the windows on both sides. But when the sun finally rose, it illuminated the sky. I woke up completely and watched the splendid view with gratitude. (Unfortunately, I didn't take any photos.)

I arrived at Chiang Mai around 1:00 pm. I went with the Canadian and Norwegian to the hostel they had booked. I decided to share a room with the Norwegian guy which was next to the woman's room. Accommodation: check! Now, beautiful Chiang Mai, it was time to check you out.

Doi Suthep

We rent two motorbikes, for 200 Baht apiece to drive to the highest temple in Chiang Mai, which was worshipped by Thai people: Wat Phrathat Doi Suthep. Before visiting the temple, I read some information about it.

I asked the Canadian: "Which bike you want to be on?"

Of course, what I really meant was who she wanted to drive with – me or the Norwegian guy. She considered and decided to choose me (^_^) because maybe I was more experienced. Indeed.

Only as we drove the Norwegian always had to stop at junctions to wait for me because I was driving like a turtle. The girl pulled my shirt: "Tam, are you really experienced? Why so slow? I laughed and told her, "You don't get it; I'm driving slowly because I am experienced!

The temple was located halfway up the mountain and the road was smooth with many wild flowers along the sides. The sunlight hardly shone through thick canopy of trees causing the cold air to become colder. I was in a short-sleeved t-shirt driving a small scooter while shivering under the skin. Every time a light shone through the clouds, I was as happy as a mom getting back from the market. And every sacrifice deserves a reward - eventually the Wat came into sight warmly and peacefully. I bought a bunch of white lotus, two candles, three incense sticks, and got down on my knees to pray.

When I recall memories of that temple, I remember the images of creamy white lotus, half-burnt incense sticks, eternally unfinished, and then long rows of bells which visitors rang one by one all afternoon... I lingered at the temple yard for a while and then left.

The mossy ramparts

It was getting late, and the bikes were running out of gas. I shut down my engine and let the bike roll on its own until the foot of the mountain – which was an interesting sight. Chiang Mai University was located in a peaceful area full of trees and year-round cool air at the foot. Another interesting observation for me here was the gas station. In Vietnam, you stop at the station, tell the person at the dispenser how much you want and they will fill the tank for you. But in Thailand, you give them the money, grab the nozzle and fill up your tank on your own. Good, huh? No need to compete with other people; no need to hold the attention of the annoyed station staff.

I carried on my way, drove around Chiang Mai, to the Square Old City surrounded by mossy walls and a moat left from the past, trying to listen for faint echoes from history.

I joined my two friends in the evening at the night market. Then, on your own, I took a tuk-tuk to a small, cheap bar crowded with people sitting around and drinking outside. Was this a place for backpackers? I wasn't sure. But I decided to stay there and had two bottles of beer to warm up my insides. I left the bar somewhere around 1:00 am. I was half-drunk in a foreign place, and had no idea how to get back. Should be quite concerned huh? Anything could happen... But that was just senseless fear – nothing would happen. A female tuk-tuk driver drove me home (She looked kind), after I gave her the address then leaned back to feel my body soak up the cool air.

Moments like this help us free our minds empty. I really thought about nothing, at all.

I came back to Chiang Mai several times after that trip. I revisited the same coldness, the same night market, the same ruined walls, and the same tranquil ancient temples. Alone in Chiang Mai, alone on its peaceful roads...

CHAPTER 5

―――――

LAOS
THE TRANQUIL BUDDHIST LAND

In my mind, I never put Laos in my bucket list. Even until the moment I started planning for the trip, I did it without much thought. So when my friend said "hey, Vietnam Airline's return ticket to Laos is only 145 USD", I was like "Oh yeah? Ok, book it". If I cancelled it last minute, it would not be a big deal.

Laos in my mind was… dense forests? Poverty? Poor adults and neglected children? The place where internet was as slow as a turtle. Power would be on and off all the times? Also, the country where people would have really dark skin. (That would be familiar to Cambodia.) Oh, and would be hundreds of people packed into old, worn-out vehicles. That was my thinking about that country. Laos was right there next to Vietnam, we shared a border, yet air tickets were ridiculously expensive. Not worth it. The more I thought about it, the more I did not feel like making a trip to Laos… but…... well, just go, create a socalled Indochina balance! By then, I had been to

Cambodia six times. And more importantly, this ticket deal was once-in-a-million years; normally, it costs 400 USD for a return ticket from Ho Chi Minh City to Vientiane.

So, let's go!

I think it must have been the world's most convoluted flight path ever. From Sai Gon, we spent two hours in transit in Phnom Penh before flying to Vientiane. Which meant not more than 45 minutes after taking off, we had to get off the plane, wait two hours in the airport, then get on the plane again. Why so hard! For just a short distance, it had to connect the biggest city in Vietnam, via the capital of a country, to the capital of another country. Just getting on and off the aircraft was already tiring enough. Fortunately, I travelled with very funny friends. We teamed up and made a crazy group, spending so much time laughing that we actually did not have enough time to get tired.

VIENTIANE

―――――

Night market

Vientiane, the capital of Laos, lied gently by the winding Mekong River. From this side of the river, one could see Nong Khai province of Thailand on the other side. Maybe on the other side, they were richer and more developed. But from here, I felt a peaceful feeling that not many places had. Every country or city had its own history.

Traditional values can become endangered when it comes to weighing historic choices with modern development. Laos was still poor, but its simple root values still gently shone on faces with sincerely kind smiles of people I met.

We arrived Vientiane when it was already night. The capital night market was already set up on this side of the river, with lights brightly illuminating an entire corner. Ha, a friend in the group, had already booked a hotel opposite the market from which the view was so great that we could see every single red marquee down the road. The whole group was excited and quickly prepared to pay a visit down there.

Honestly, I hadn't looked forward to anything from this country; "The land of a million elephants". I just wanted to spend time with my weirdos. Within our group, only Ha had previously lived in Laos as a volunteer for a children's project. The rest of us followed along. Thankfully, Ha was a considerate person who took care of what we ate, where we stayed – literally everything.

Vientiane's night market spread out to a fairly wide area, but wasn't too crowded. It was well organized and not too noisy like some other markets. The products were mainly handcrafts from Laos, clothes and others made in China (Just like every market in Asia and around the world).

The first thing I bought was something that no one expected: a slingshot. Slingshots were something that closely connected to my Vietnamese childhood. As a child, I would spend all day playing around mounds and fields with neighbours with slingshots ready in our hands; waiting for birds to shoot. It was an experience impossible to erase from memory. So the moment the kiosk with the slingshot came into my sight, it triggered the feeling of being a boy again with a target in sight, and I bought the toy weapon without thinking. Not to shoot at anything anymore, just as a keepsake to hang in my room. Over time, as life and all of its mediocre distractions keep us busy, we all begin to forget those sweet memories. So now there are many items in my room: a mask bought in Venice, a Mona Lisa souvenir portrait bought from the Louvre museum, an ancient coin from Notre-Dame de Paris, a Starbucks mugs bearing a white horse from Chiang Mai among others. (Sometimes I wonder if I was an ant in a previous life; carrying stuff to its home.) My friends have a hard time understanding the purpose of these weird things in my room. This time, again, I tried to explain to them my choice. It's just that every time I see those souvenirs from faroff places, the memories that happened during those trips come back into my mind. It's a feeling of sweetness.

We chose a place highly recommended by TripAdvisor for the meal. Ha told us Lao food was the best but no one believed her. How could that be possible? Laos was not on the world food map! However, after a couple of days, Ha proved us all wrong. Chicken, fish, vegetables, coconuts, fruits, wild boar, BBQ - even if you're travelling as a backpacker, save for your budget on accommodation, transportation, save this or that, but don't save on food – the food must be good. Why? We eat to have the energy to go around, to enjoy the food culture of a country, and to live.

Night on the long road

Vientiane by night was gentle. Quiet streets covered by shadows of big trees, as if they were peacefully sleeping. Just a short walk from the hotel, I came upon to the sight of ancient darkcolored temples half illuminated under yellow street lights. Echoing in the air was the whisper of chants. Some street vendors for food and drinks targeting Westerner backpackers were still open but it wasn't too noisy, or crowded, everything operated smooth and mild.

We returned to the night market around 10 pm. Surprisingly, it looked as if there had never been a night market; the whole area was now just an empty, grey cement yard, gusty from the winds blowing up from the Mekong River. We were surprised; we didn't think that the market would wrap up so fast. The whole town was now closed and empty.

I guessed it was time for bed…

This morning

The first morning in Vientiane I was startled by an unbelievably pure scene: the glorious morning sunshine, bathed the town in a greenish light through the leaves of the massive old trees which were so big that it would take several people holding hands to barely reach around them. I saw temples overlaid in gold gleaming under the sunshine, along clean and clear streets. My vision before of a poor and ugly Laos vanished, making room for another Laos which was new and gorgeous. Even the Lao people were not as dark as in my imagination – they were same as in Vietnam: not too bright, not too dark, but with typical Asian brown skin. I was impressed by the older ladies who looked uncommonly kind. We visited hundred-year-old temples like the bright golden Pha That Luang, the sacred Haw Phra Kaew with time stamped on green moss, Wat Si Saket. We went to the Patuxai Victory Gate proudly located in the center to have a panoramic sight over this peaceful little green town. Then we leisurely relaxed in the afternoon in a nondescript temple.

I would never call these days my travelling days. They were simply days when I truly lived. And I was lucky to live such peaceful days with no worries in a foreign city, surrounded by a foreign language, with good food and dear friends. Trips without purpose are simply days walking leisurely in town, watching people, listening their language, appreciating their smiles. That is all. Nothing big. Or maybe just days sitting quiet and sad in the garden of a certain temple, listening to chants flying with the wind into the tree canopies and then bleeding out over the open space. There are days visiting foreign cities, in which I put aside busy days in Saigon, to feel the culture, people, and free myself to welcome new things, and eventually, to remove prejudgments of places where I have never been.

Leaving Vientiane on a morning bus, I arrived Vang Vieng – a place where I had been urged to come by afternoon through smoky mountains.

VANG VIENG

———

Organic Farm

With every step we take, the world opens up in front
of us with many more beautiful things to see...

Vang Vieng is a town with very small center – so tiny that when we walked around at night, we kept seeing the same fellow backpackers again and again! It was a good thing, we did not stay in the center. Thanks to Ha, who used to volunteer here, we were lead to a farm called Organic Farm[8]. This was not just a normal farm with cattle, goats, chickens, sericulture and planting crops. There was a noble mission behind Organic. This was a volunteer organization which aimed at connecting community and support people with opportunities.

Organic Farm was located on a very favorable position for enjoying Lao's peaceful landscape. The farm was by the Nam Song River which was flowing sluggishly while we were there, while on the bank of the other side sat imposing limestone hills, gigantic and

---

8   *For more information about Organic Farm, visit http://www.laofarm.org/*

enchanting. Later we found that the river dock by Organic Farm was a site for many sporting events, sightseeing, and adventure activities on the Nam Song River. The overnight rate at Organic farm was pretty friendly to backpackers at only $15 USD/double room and the food was charming. Food was unusual and organic, including such options as: fried eggs with crispy mulberry leaves, wild bamboo soup which still retained its bitterness, boiled vegetables, crispy goat cheese, and papaya salad. We had these staples with red rice and kept on praising the food and praising Ha to thank her for leading us to such a feast – tastes which completely fit the Vietnamese palate. We continued eating until everybody was engorged.

I remember the mornings when I would wake up and take a leisurely breakfast in shelters by the river, looking at the silky-like dew drop tail spinning above the water. Life moved slowly and leisurely. Our group rolled up trousers to wade into the river taking photos. Then we put on life-jackets and hopped on a big inner tube, just lying on it to enjoy the sky and white clouds. In the afternoons, we'd go again to the dock to play in the water and watch the clouds drifting over the mountains.

If you have chance to visit Vang Vieng, I whole-heartily recommend Organic Farm. Check it out.

The world's most peaceful town

Vang Vieng doesn't have many activities at night, while in the daytime, it is a sport center with interesting things to do outdoors. If you are river-lover, then this place is for you; you can drift along slowly on an inner tube on the dreamy Nam Song river. Over 4km of free floating, no one else but you, the sky, the water, clouds, mountains, and forests. You just lie there doing nothing, worrying about nothing. The river is as gently kind as its people. If you don't like to float, you can also go with a kayak at a higher speed. Or if you are a mountain person, how about an adventure like climbing, mountain biking or caving? Along both sides of the river are natural caves, many of which are still untouched. Also on the Nam Song river, there are beer places which tempt you into dropping by to enjoy a fresh, cold Beer Lao. We had the best papaya salad in the world in one of these places, awfully spicy and wonderfully delicious at the same time.

When we stumbled over a group of people who wanted to explore a nearby cave, we joined them. The cave was totally natural, completely dark. We had to swim over a cold and wild area of water to get into the cave but once inside, we were rendered speechless. It was brilliant with sparkling stalactites. We shared a limited number of flashlights with each other to show the way in that dark and sticky-mudded place. The floor was really slippery; I had a painful fall which left a red gash on my leg that has become a scar. (I named it "Scar of Vang Vieng" – cute, huh?) Then it came the time to leave

Vang Vieng for Xiang Khoang to see the Plain of Jars. Still in love with the sunset over the river, I decided to stay Vang Vieng for a few more days on my own. I moved to a small hostel in the center, rented a bicycle, then cycled fast to the bus station to see my friends off. After three hours of speedy cycling, welcoming me was just an empty bus station – there was no sign of my frolicking gang. They had left. Unexplained sadness.

But that feeling lasted just a moment, like when we first stepped out of a party. I cycled back to the town really slowly because no one was waiting for me ahead. I was leisurely enjoying the road winding along the river, watching the sun set little by little behind the mountains. Smoke went up from kitchens, birds hurriedly flew back to their nests in the last sun rays of the day, dazzling pink clouds gathered at a corner of the sky, quiet space as if you were already far far away from the busy town...but in truth, you were still in the middle of town. It was not easy to feel this in Sai Gon. You could even bring your favorite book to a river shelter and read, enjoy a bottle of Beer Lao and listen to the sound of water flowing under your feet. Days were slow here, as you can see. This tranquility was typical of Laos. Everywhere I went, people were quiet, tranquil, and kind just like that.

Morning was slow, noon was slow, and it was not different in the afternoon. Of course, night was extremely long. I wandered around and shortly covered the tiny town. Even the faces of my fellow backpackers looked familiar; I met them again and again at every corner as in Vientiane. Lao people gave me strange looks - maybe it was because I looked similar and yet not-similar to them. Perhaps there weren't so many Vietnamese travellers there?

I walked alone, gloomy, lonely, slowly, leisurely, as if the Vang Vieng afternoon was already inside of me; I opened myself to invite the afternoon to gently walk into my heart.

I call Vang Vieng the most peaceful town on the Earth and I think no one can disagree.

Leaving Vang Vieng

One day when I woke up, I realized Vang Vien was beautiful yet too sleepy to stay alone here for many days. I decided to catch a bus to the most famous city of Laos: Luang Prabang. As planned (If I had a really good plan), I could across the Golden Triangle from Luang Prabang, to Chiang Rai, then down to Chiang Mai, from there fly to Bangkok and then head back to Saigon. I did have that kind of intention. But it might change.

The six-and-a-half-hour bus costed $13 USD. Most of the passengers were Westerner backpackers, that day there was a Asian backpacker in short and flip-flop sitting next to the driver. We arrived at a bus stop halfway down hills. I had never been to any bus stop that were with so much fresh air and beautiful landscape.

Endless mountain ranges were there far away, flowers bloomed over the pathway, clouds were slowly floating right over the head...

However, the road was quite concerned. Not like Vietnam, a majority geographic area of Laos was made up of mountain ranges and highlands and forest. They had night bus, but deep down I avoided it due to risks. Seriously. Well, day bus would be tiring due to curves, high latitude roads along endless mountains, but it was safer. With such geography, no matter how big it is, the national agriculture and industry cannot develop, they even do not have sea ports for foreign trade, it's easy to understand why Laos is still poor.

However, poor but happy. I can feel that clearly during days I was travelling in this country. Eventually, all people want for life is happiness, isn't it? If Lao people have iPhone, iPad, television per person, it doesn't mean they would be happy or their traditional value would be preserved. If so, one day, they will go to bars instead of pagodas, to supermarkets instead of local markets. Which one is better? Every choice has its price. Personally, as a traveler, I hope Laos could stay the same, maintain its typical. That's what creates diversity among countries, among cities. Cities are special just because they have their own cultural typical which you can find at nowhere in the world.

That is why even it's Asian, it's Buddhist, and its economy has not been developed yet, Luang Prabang still has its soul that charms all the travellers.

LUANG PRABANG

————

Homestay

The bus stopped at the beginning of the central night market. In the afternoon. Right here, just a little bit later, there would be a bustling night market.

All passengers got off the bus and left, there were only four people left: me, an Australian girl and two French guys. The Aussie girl asked the two guys where they would stay and how much that place could be. She shrugged her shoulders and left after commented "Too expensive".

She then suddenly turned her head and asked me "Hey Tam, wanna join me find a place for us?". Well, why not? Actually, I already knew her when I was in Vang Vien, we talked a bit while there. And that was how we ended up going to Luang Prabang together on same bus. The French jumped onto motorbike of a local guy and disappeared into the city. Looking at the poor small motorbike carrying 3 guys with two French giants, we felt pity for it. The girl and I left the station with our backpacks.

"Hey Tam, I will just want a cheap place, like 10-12 USD per night. You know what, I paid 7 dollars for the place in Vang Vien."

I secretly thought "man, what a good bargain she made considering she is Aussie". In Vang Vien I paid 15 dollars for a single room. Of course, I didn't tell her what I really thought. I hummed and hawed to everything she said.

Anyway, the room rate in Luang Prabang was not cheap at all, especially places looking not bad around river's area, almost minimum 50 dollars. We walked until our legs got exhausted. Then we arrived a tiny homestay opposite to Wat Xieng Thong, 20 dollars per day. It was a house locating on a short slope, there were many flowers in front and run by a middle-age lady with kind face. The Australian girl, of course, didn't want that price. I had to leave with her. Walked a bit more, there was another house with 15 dollars, but there were a bunch of young guys standing in front and the rooms were not clean. It was the time I knew that we should separate here. She said:

"Tam, I think 15 dollars should be OK for you. I'll find something cheaper for me."

I quickly agreed, and waited until she left, I backed to the place with 20 dollars. Not sure why I used my money but felt like stolen money. Honestly, I didn't want her to feel bad. I was afraid she would judge that Vietnamese was poor but lavish. Although the rate was pretty high, but my room was excellent in a kind family, which was great. I met the girl again at the night market. She told me she had spent one more hour and found a hostel with 12 dollars.

Too expensive but I thought it was the cheapest here already. (Well, everybody wants cheap, of course, but I really don't want to wake up the following day and have nothing to wear)

Where time stands still

The homestay was on a small road opposite to Wat Xieng Thong, right in the night market area. Every morning, when the last dew drop fell out of the grass by the side of the road, I slowly woke up, dressed up and left the place. The road passing by Wat Xieng Thong was fulfilled with whispers of chants. I went to the end of the ancient quarter, bought breakfast then got down on my knees, just like everybody else, with the eyes full of peace and contentment, despite being locals or travellers. If anyone ever know about Luang Prabang or ever travelled there, all would agree that one of the most beautiful things happening every morning is the alms giving ceremony. As the sun rose in Luang Prabang, when the sun shone its first light on the stone road: monks depart from their temples to gather their daily meal. I and many people with orange scarves kneeled down by the roadside, respectfully gave our offering to the monks. The line was long, must be at least hundreds of monks dressing in their dark-orange robes. The age of monks got younger and younger along the line. Novices at the end, though still being young, their steps were already deliberate and at peace and calm. In this offering moment, I deeply felt moved. The world out there seemed not to exist, envy and competition became nonsense. During that sacred ceremony, only tranquility covered the whole space and time. Every morning, lines of monks kept going, in order, absolutely quiet, walked by the ancient roads, passed by hundredyear-old temples. That long orange line would disappear when the sun went up and the morning began, people then stood up, wrapped up things and returned to their things. That was Luang Prabang, I called it the place where time stands still.

How can we find such undisturbed and tranquil paradise among this busy life?

I found the answer to this question later at night, while walking around the night market, the power was suddenly off, everything was quietly sunk in darkness. When power came back, everybody resumed their work as if during the power cut they had been frozen like in a fiction movie. No scream, no laugh, no kid's sound, no complain, etc. Nothing! Even when being asked for price, they gently took the calculators and typed the price, mildly smiled. Buying or not, didn't matter, the smile was still there. There was something close about the smiles. Noise was something strange and weird in life of local people. They were quiet, paid honour to Buddha and they were divine.

The lady who owned the homestay was above 50, pretty and kindhearted. She had a daughter who was at secondary and a son who was helping her to run the place. Once day, I asked her where to rent a bike or a bicycle to go around. She couldn't speak English, so did her daughter while the son who could speak good English was not at home. I used my hands to mimic the action of riding a bike, she shook her head. I pointed outside which I meant to ask if there was any place for that in the area. She nodded her head. Then I made my feet as if I was riding a bicycle, then her face was shining, nodding her head. Then she said something to her daughter. The girl ran to the back of the house and brought along a pink bicycle. I tried to ask them how much I should pay, she shook her head and smiled nicely. Which meant "It's free". The girl showed me how to lock the bike, wished me a good day then went back to help her mother with cooking. That pink bike helped me to go around during days in Luang Prabang.

The town was not big, just some rounds then I could cover all of it already, but it seemed that I never got enough of it. I cycled around and around, to the market buying some souvenirs, to the small roads where there was a school and students who always made a pleasant noise, to museum or temples, to a familiar coffee shop by the river, etc. There was not any sound remaining in my mind during days staying here except the chants. The chants filled up the air in early mornings, at noon, at twilights and even in silent nights, etc.

And in Luang Prabang, there were many pink bicycles, I realized such after walking out of a coffee shop. The bikes were manufactured by one company, same colour, same design. I had to try unlocking every single one to find mine. Learn from the fact, I tied a band on the front basket to mark it. Fortunately, it was weekend, the girl did not go to school, so I could use the pink bike the whole time, cycled here, cycled there.

Two days later, my friends arrived. I still stayed at the homestay because I so much liked it. But had to ride to my friends 'hotel every morning to meetup with them. The meetup place was the famous coffee shop named Utopia. The place located deep in an alley, but once you got there, the scene was awesome. It was by the Nam Khan river in dry season, the wind blew gently making our heart feel easy. The coffee shop was designed open, with many pillows and mattress of Laos style. Customers could sit or lie or stand – whatever they wanted to. I and my friends spent the time there playing cards, reading books. There were times we overslept due to the gentle dearly wind.

In this scene, we could do whatever. What could we want more? In lazy days, we just went to the place, lying there just to relax, then ordered food when hungry (their food was pretty good). After that, we went to the night market when it was dark, eating everything from papaya salad, to grilled fish, chicken wings, sticky rice, etc. An interesting thing was we could meet all familiar faces who we used to meet in previous towns, and chat.

Luang Prabang was just that simple. If you wanted to fi nd something joyful after ten in Luang Prabang, I don't think it would be possible. It would already sink into silence by then. I went back to the homestay, stopped a bit by the ancient temple looking at the empty streets, empty market, feeling the breeze and hearing the endless chants.

To me, Luang Prabang would always be in my heart with such tranquility.

Fisher man in the Inle Lake, Myanmar

Cycling in the Summer time, Bagan, Myanmar

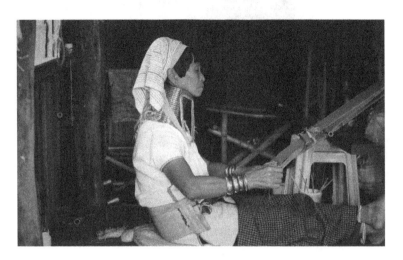

A long-neck woman working with the loom, Inle Lake, Myanmar

A smiling face, Myanmar

A young monk shopping for groceries, Yangon, Myanmar

The sound of horse's hoofs at dusk

On the top of the hill, Cameron Highland, Malaysia

Get lost in Angkor, Cambodia

A peaceful Angkor at dawn, Cambodia

Daily scene in Myanmar

Monk procession in early morning, Luang Prabang, Laos

Inside an ancient Pagoda, Laos

An old town, Luang Prabang, Laos

With friends Pip and Thuy on Nam Song river, Vang Vieng, Laos

Ancient Pagodas in Chiang Mai, Thailand

The Buddha temple in Ayutthaya, Thailand

A Souvernier shop in Chiang Mai, Thailand

A rainy day in Bangkok, Thailand

PART II

A LITTLE BIT FURTHER

CHAPTER 6

PACKED IN HONGKONG

After some short trips to near places like Phnom Penh, Bangkok, Singapore, Kuala Lumpur, etc. I ventured to travel to Hongkong, alone. Maybe, people think it is so easy to go to Hongkong, but to me at that time, it took my braveness to do so. The city was strange and living expense was high. Air tickets were expensive. Moreover, it was not easy to apply for Hongkong visa.

Hong Kong Airport was like a maze which I must pay hard attention not to get lost, had to use train to travel from this terminal to that terminal, then caught the free shuttle to the city. To a guy who knew nothing like me, it was already too much. Every time I knew I was in the right direction, I felt happy. How good I was, haha.

Hong Kong welcomed me with a shower, not too big but for a long time. Hong King had so many high buildings, as a result, its rain was weird, it was vertical and not much windy. If you looked up, you really could see how a rain drop fell until it was broken down to the ground. During rainy season, there was always an umbrella in the bag of Hong Kong people. Once it started to rain, the whole city would be filled up with colorful umbrellas. The streets became wet but looked really playful with moving "Round objects".

The wheeled-case in one hand, I covered my head with the backpack and squeezed my way through people. "Why too many people? Where I am going?" – Honestly, I was a bit lost then. But whatever, have to find the accommodation first. I was not really sure where it was, I just knew it was on Nathan road. There was no house number in Hong Kong, but I figured out later that they listed numbers of houses at the junctions, which meant from here would be houses numbered blah blah blah. But in those first hours in Hong Kong, I didn't know where to find. I asked locals, but they rid me of. Well, maybe because it was early morning.

Luckily, there was an Indian old man who knew the place. He told me to go to the opposite side, walk a bit more. There I went. But! Oh My Gosh, broken, scared, disappointed. Oh gosh, all bad words I knew appeared in my head at that moment.

Elevators were used for specific floors, one for odd numbers and one for even numbers. There were many elevators in the building and they didn't connect with each other. Another bad thing: this was Indian building. As a result, it was too smelly. When I still had my job at HSBC and ANZ banks, honestly, I didn't like Indian colleagues, they had curry smell which was kinda unpleasant. Hic...

I guessed the owner of my hostel would be an Indian, but no, it was a black American. He had 3 long scars on his face and he was looking askance at me. He was wearing a low-rise hip-hop pants, he was not only dark but also full of tattoos. I, to be honest, felt insecure.

I wondered if my luggage would be safe while I was out? I brought many good stuff with me this time :(((C'mon, it was superb Hong Kong, I thought I should look cool, right?)

The black American guy checked the book and "no vacancy", haha… well, even I pre-paid 10% of the rate, there was no room for me. I also managed to look at the book, many Vietnamese were staying here. Maybe because it was cheap here? He said, "Never mind, follow me downstairs". What was waiting for me downstairs, I was curious?

Well, fortunately, downstairs was a Philippines lady who looked kinda nice with a son who has a curly hair. She cleaned the room and welcomed me. I had never seen any hotel room that was that ridiculously small. It was an old apartment, they separated it into many smaller rooms for rent. Was this Hong Kong? Really? But… anyway, as long as it was clean, I should be fine. Let's just have a good sleep and discover it! The journey began!

My very first feeling for Hong Kong was shopping. Stores were everywhere. My hostel was on Nathan Road, which was the busiest in Hong Kong in general and in Tsim Sha Tsui (Chinese: 尖沙咀) in particular. Walking out of the building, there were shops on the right, shops on the left, shops in front of you. Everywhere. And goods were much cheaper than in Singapore, Bangkok or Vietnam (Of course). Because goods in Hong Kong were duty-free, so I shopped like crazy. Not to mention promotion programs that every store offered at that moment.

I left the hostel at ten in the morning, went to a G2000 store to buy shirts. I left the store at noon with many shopping bags in my hands. A Bossini store was also on their last day of sale, customers were packed inside. I thought if I went to have lunch then come back later, there would be nothing left for me to buy. I hold my hunger to sneak into the store. I got out of it at two in the after. I went to find something to eat worrying that I would die of hunger on the way. So, before I could find something to eat, I bought a Hong Kong milk tea and water to keep myself alive. As a result, I didn't feel good after I had a dish of chicken fried rice. I prayed to Buddha that I could arrive the hostel safely before anything shame could happen due to that full stomach. Luckily, nothing bad happened. I saved my face!!!

There was another feeling: hard to breath. Streets were packed with people. Walking by foot didn't mean leisure while in Hong Kong. We should keep eyes straight to the front to make sure you would not hit anybody.

I went to the Ladies Market, but just entered two kiosks and stepped back immediately. It was unbearable: could not breathe and so lonely that I had never felt before every time I travelled alone. The extreme loneliness. I didn't get it. I always chose to travel alone to feel the place, and this was definitely not the first time I was solo. I was fully confident that I know how to entertain myself while backpacking. However, this time in Hong Kong, among this awful crowd, it made me felt completely lonely. This kind of atmosphere would be much better if I had travelled with friends. That moment, I swore that if I ever returned here, it would not be me alone.

The crowded streets created a busy life in Hongkong with tall buildings. It was said that Hong Kong residents being forced to live on top of each other, up to the sky. It was one hundred percent correct. You would always feel like you were too small among skyscrapers which were as tall as the eyes could see. Beautiful girls were wrapped in cigarette smoke with LV bags in hands and spoke English like native. Young men with shirts covered with light vests. There was a fact to be agreed that Hong Kong style was well-being, sporty but smartly. They didn't make it too much like anywhere else.

People also walked so fast. I was known among my friends that I was a fast walker, but here in Hong Kong, my speed was nothing. Maybe because walking was their habit. They had to walk a lot. It took at least fifteen minutes to walk from a subway station to the nearest one, half walk half run. If you were not used to doing exercise or you were not a strong one, you may not be able to handle this. I breathed so hard while walking in Hong Kong even I was famous for my long legs.

Hong Kong made an impression on me with smoke and fast walkers, the feeling of loneliness in the sea of people, and the void in heart that was unable to be filled. The thoughts of solitude were undeniable. I had thought I would come back at year-end, but definitely not going alone.

CHAPTER 7

JAPAN

T alking about Asia, people always think of cities with strong taste of culture, small villages with kids who have clear eyes, or beautiful routes that charm traveler's soul. However, there is another Asia with Japan, Korea, Hong Kong and Singapore – I personally call it the developed Asia. And there is a common denominator of these developed places: busy people, fast walkers, skyscrapers, stylish boys and girls on streets with cigarettes in their hands, luxury restaurants and bars, busy networks of metro lines like spider's webs stretching out from an end to the other end of the city.

The prejudgment misleads people. Until one day when I visited Japan, I concluded that Japan was so much special that it becomes unique. We cannot mistake it with any other.

Days I was alone in the city of silence...

TOKYO
THE CITY OF SILENCE

———

Start

The night flight made me tired. I was kinda easy to sleep, no matter where I was, on train or plane. But the reason why this flight departing at 7:00 pm and arriving at Tokyo at 7:30 am made me unable to sleep was I flew with Malaysia Airlines. The haunting of MH370 and the following scandals of this Airlines made not only me, but other passengers feel a bit nervous. The outside was pitch-black. Every time we entered a turbulence, I held fast to the seat with my fingers and kept on being nervous. But why did I choose the Malaysia Airlines anyway? Simply, incredibly cheap tickets! I didn't fly Sai Gon – Narita round trip. My itinerary was Saigon – Narita and then back to Saigon from Osaka. I had been so worried that I even purchased travel insurance without a second of hesitation.

Until when I was writing this, MH17 incident was shocking the whole world. From the fatal date of MH17, guess everybody who flew with Malaysia Airlines would be double nervous though financial reasons always pushed people to make unfavourable decision.

Destiny – the only word that can describe the meaning of the roads one takes.

Nobody knows what is waiting ahead…

In the morning I landed in Narita airport, I breathed a sigh of relief after getting through a night of nervous. Although I would be flying with Malaysia Airlines again on the long flight back, just enjoy the moment. Narita airport was huge and in order. But I did not make sound of excitement anymore. I quickly finished immigration process and headed to the city via metro line. Until then, I hadn't booked hotel. I thought I would stay with Mr. Okamura. Visiting Japan and staying in a homestay had been my dreams. No, not only Japan, I always try to stay with local wherever I go. So that I could learn their culture, way of living, taste their foods and "Be there" as a local, see their country the way they see. And not to mention, save costs. Who can dislike such?

Talking about Okamura, he was my customer in Vietnam. When I asked whom I should ask for information while in Tokyo, he warmly offered help. He told me to take a bus in the afternoon and stop at the station, he would pick me up. Of course, I could not stay the whole day in the airport to wait until the afternoon. I went to downtown first, I was eager to know the legendary Tokyo.

But, taking the city line was not simple as it's said to be. Ticket of Japan Railways was a problem. It was in Japanese and just a few English which was not enough to understand. I had zero knowledge of Japanese and Japanese's English was already famous for…well, we all know, English speakers were not really welcomed. Luckily,

I managed to find the correct train, got on it, sat in my seat (After wrongly sat on people's seat). I went to Shinjuku ward with my big case and backpack. I walked out of the metro station looking at the busy streets while the sleepiness was coming. It was 9:00 am in Japan and but just 7:00 am in Vietnam – still too early for me at home. Tokyo here I come…

Kabukicho

I remembered that day, the first location I checked-in was Kabukicho. C'mon, I had no idea about that area. I opened the phone, it showed the location, I checked in, that was it. My friends altogether chatted: hey, you have real balls huh? You just arrived Japan and you go there immediately? – What the hell? I didn't understand. Kabukicho looked boring, it was empty. There was nothing fun now?

It was until later that I knew the reason: I was standing in the middle of the wildest Red-light district in Japan, even in the whole world.

But "Red light" was the story of the night. Now, it was day time, Kabukicho was just like any other quiet streets in Japan, only some stores were open and could not unseen the run-down status of corner. The notorious Shinjuku, Kabukicho was just only this? To be honest, I was a bit disappointed considering I was having handful of luggage and sleepless and hungry. The only wish at that moment:

sleep. I needed a place to lie down and sleep to recharge myself for the coming discovery. But I knew that I couldn't wait until 6pm to come to the Okamura's in this condition. Fortunately, before I went, Quan had given me the address of a capsule hostel he used to stay, discount voucher and a Lonely Planet. Briefly, all useful information for now! I headed to find the hostel.

Pupa

Accommodation in Tokyo was super expensive, more than ones in USA and Europe where I used to stay. They were so expensive that they had to develop the capsule model which was enough for just one person lying down or sit up, meaning a normal hotel room could be divided into many capsules, each for one person. All other activities: shower, laundry, luggage, etc. were all in common areas.

There were many things to tell about showering. In Vietnam, those things should be private, no one does such in common places shared with many people. However, here, not only shared with many people, it would happen in front of everybody. If I really wanted to think positive, "Everybody does that", no one cared. Anyway, it was a bit awkward telling about this, I would skip back to the part when I was looking for the hostel.

After nearly two hours, I finally found it (It was pretty confused to find houses in Japan though I had address in hand). I was super happy when I found it after hours of dragging my luggage around. Walking in and smiling nicely with the receptionist, I was welcomed the same with a smile from a cute girl who then asked me, "Do you have tattoo?". I, with the typical honesty of Southern Vietnamese, said "Yes, but tiny!" (Actually, not tiny). The girl didn't change her nice attitude but started to excuse, "I apologize, my place has rules that we don't accept guests with tattoos. You can check the rules over there." Then she pointed to a big board. "I truly apologize; I am sorry…"

The big board in the middle of the lobby said that "Guests with tattoos or tattoo-like paintings on body would not be accepted!" I sadly left the place. Later, my friend told me that area was raged by Yakuza mafia, so locals were really scared of people who had tattoo.

After that, I figured out not only that area, but all public bath houses in Japan had the same rules, as if they tried to tell you "Hey, if you have tattoos, sneak yourself into a private place, don't scare other people." This is the modern Tokyo? Really? Tattoo was a fashion these days, wasn't it? I walked out knowing nothing I could do next.

I left the capsule hostel with the obsessing tattoo, I thought if the next hostel asked that question, I should say "No", that I was a tattoo virgin. With my backpacking experience, I quickly found another capsule hostel, also in Shinjuku. The first thing was to check if their rules board said something about tattoos. Gladly, nope.

Finding that hostel was another story. I walked by it like 20 times before but didn't see it. I was bad, I know, but shouldn't be it there right on the street? I kept passing, passing and still couldn't find it.

Japan was a strange nation. In Vietnam and I think all other countries in the world, business means being in front. All other hidden parts like office or accommodation, can be upstairs or behind, wherever, but business means the front. While in Japan, it was not the same. Ground floor would be restaurant, second floor would be another restaurant, third floor or fourth floor would be again another restaurant or a coffee shop, etc. Therefore, all my photos I took at night in Japan, guess what you would see? Only neon signs, full of them. Yes, every single floor would be place for such. Thus, if you wanna find a place, you should really pay attention and check every single sign boards. It happened many times, when I used Google Maps, I thought I already arrived where I wanted to be. But for unknown reason, I still couldn't find it. I had to have my eyes work so hard to read boards which were 80% Japanese and 20% English from ground to top.

Same with the hostel I wanna check. After being tired of walking around, I decided to try asking an old man in neighbour building. He immediately got what I wanted. A young guy having luggage in hands, he must be looking for a cheap capsule hostel. He told me to follow him, then he crossed the street, and showed me to turn left into the 9-storey building, then used elevator to Floor 4th which was the hostel reception. I looked around to see if I missed anything, because I could not find the place. Suddenly, I noticed a very small sign jumbled up with many other boards of beer places, restaurants, karaoke. Oh gosh! What kind of hostel that had its reception on 4th floor? How you expect people to find you, huh? To be honest, I was a bit upset.

It was 2:00 pm that time. The receptionist after asking me for information, she advised to book online, for a better rate. But one more issue, I could only check-in after 4:00 pm. Oh man, now I knew their check-in checkout time: checkout before 10:00 am and check-in after 4:00 pm. All guests must check out before 10 every day no matter how long they stay. They can go everywhere then can only return after 4:00 pm. One good point: we can leave luggage in the hostel. If they refused to keep my luggage, I would just die.

So, yeah, every day, no matter how tired I was, 10 o'clock, leave! The thing I hate the most was being woken up while sleeping, here in Tokyo, puh… oh Tokyo…

Hard days

So, I checked in, left the luggage and went out with the backpack of valuable stuff. Valuable things consisted of MacBook Air, iPad, Canon camera, water, hard drive, book, some stuff, etc. all weighted about 7 to 9 kilos. Every day, like farmer woke up for the field, at 10:00 am, I carried about 7 – 9 kilos on my shoulder, walked around Tokyo. Then I went back at about 8 pm, sweating the whole body.

I called days in Tokyo were heavy work-out days. It was hard but no time to rest. If I was tired, I would just sit down on the floor of a station, and rested, waited until got better and continued to go. It was always like that, from here to there. Water bought from vending machines, food from some street vendors, travelled far distance by train. The days kept on being like that. Even right now when I was writing this, still felt so real those days.

I nearly lost my feeling for walking due to long walking. There were times when I almost missed my step. My shoulders also became painful due to carrying to the heavy backpack. That moment, the backpack was like a damn thing that I could not throw away. It was Vietnamese way of thinking: where you are, there your things. But after some days in Japan, I knew that it was time for me to change my thinking a bit, ah no, a lot.

In Japan, vending machines were everywhere. There was another thing that were always there in public places like metro stations, airport or crowded placed: the coin locker. Coin locker was a locker in public place, you insert coins, open the locker, put your things in, lock it then you can go anywhere, after that you go back and collect your things. At the beginning, I thought, "is it safe? Would be an empty locker waiting for me when I'm back?". Excuse me, I was born in a country with bad reputation of such public habit. It was not my fault, right? Sorry!

Some days later, I really could not handle the backpack the whole day. I decided to take my risk, I put my things in a locker at the station near the hotel. But it was not the point! I could carry my backpack until I died because I was worried to lose my things. But once I dared to leave my valuable stuff in a strange place, there must

---

be just for one reason: I trusted! My trust for Japanese was growing every single day, through people I met on street, from what I saw, by times I asked for help, from how they operated every day in such a busy society. I had a strong belief that no one would steal my things. And if there were any bad guy who really did so, Japanese police and camera surveillance and locals would never ever allow such to happen. If I talk about Japanese, I would write about them in another topic. But I must say those ordinary people never fail to surprise me in admiration.

One small detail, after I checked in the hotel, I figured out that it was impossible for me to stay at the Okamura's. His place was one hour by bus from Tokyo, it was not polite of me if I always disturb them by going home late at night every day. It would bother also. With this kind of transportation system, if someone couldn't speak Japanese, there was really potential to sleep on the street (because it was not easy to find ways). I texted to apologize Mr. Okamura and we would meet later in Sai Gon.

In the city of quietness

So, those were the days in Tokyo. I visited temples, Shinjuku, Shibuya, Harajuku, Ginza... I used metro lines to traverse Tokyo. I got more and more used to Japanese names. And I made friends with the quietness...

I couldn't imagine that, since the day I can speak, it was the longest time I didn't talk, at all. Days in Tokyo, I was like melted into the city. I threw myself into the busy crowd on streets, felt like these people rolled out from boxes of balls. Melted, mixed, quiet, excited, and happy.

I was warned before the trip about Japanese who couldn't speak English. I actually was not worried much about it, because language was not the only way. There were many other ways for human communication. It was also said that Chinese cannot speak English but I myself had Shanghai friends who speak perfect English. So, yeah, sometimes, "I heard" does not mean it is true. So, I believed that young Japanese may speak English to me. Anyway, this time I was a bit unlucky. There were times I got lost, after hearing me saying "Excuse me", people immediately smiled and said "Sorry". That surely didn't mean that they refused to help me, but it meant they would not understand what I was going to say. However, there were still many people though couldn't speak English but were still willing to help, they tried all ways until they couldn't.

But, another but, things were not too bad. It was not that Japanese completely couldn't speak English. Just don't ask them long question or use difficult English, point to the map and say the name of the place, then they can help you. They can say simple hello, using simple English to show direction, and other simple conversation. I think, it was enough already. I didn't go to Japan to find someone to talk to me about the universe or the life theories. What I needed was just

"How to get to that park?" "Does this line go to or pass by ABCD?" "Where is H&M, please?" That was it. Simple turned out to be good.

Also, Japanese themselves are famous for less talk. The whole nation speaks less, slow, small like whispers. Streets were crowded but it was rare to hear people talk on the way or baby cries or parent's complaints. Not to mention, no vehicle noise or street music.

There was only the sound of crows on roofs, the sound of trees shaking with the wind in a quiet afternoon. The first time I was on Tokyo subway, to my surprise, the whole train which was full of people after work or students after school was really quiet or just with very small sound. Among those people, no one wanted to bother others. As if they froze themselves waiting until their turn to get off. I noticed small kids at about 7 or 8 years old, got on the subway, found their places then started reading manga. They were quiet until the subway reached their station, they were not like kids in my country who were playful noisily all the times. If they were taught that way since young, they would grow up and respect other's space and quietness, they would know how to behave, know the common sense and how to be humble.

Loving Japan

Yes, Japanese are humble. Even during the Tohoku tsunami in 2011 which caused 15,854 deaths, 9,677 injured and 3,155 missing in 18 provinces and partly or completely destroyed 125,000 buildings, Japanese still orderly stood in queue waiting for evacuation and received governmental aids. Even when their families died or unable to be found, they still hid their tears patiently waited, they didn't make a mess. Even when they lost over Golden Coast in the World Cup, their supporters still stayed after the match to collect garbage on the stadium.

In mornings, both young and old would wore polite suits, walked to the subway. Long time before this trip, one day I read an article saying that Japanese Prime Minister went to work by subway, I (ashamedly) didn't really appreciate. I thought there would be about eight hundred reporters running behind him taking photos? But after coming here, seeing how their society worked, I realized that Prime Minister taking subway to work was not strange at all.

My pre-trip thoughts (About tattoos, sex, their wildness) were completely changed after being here. It would be rare seeing a girl in exposed dressing even during summer days. But they dared to express. If there are 10 Japanese standing in front of you, for sure you would see 10 different styles. "be different to survive" – that was what I felt. In my country, if someone is different, he would be the target of criticism. But in Tokyo, they love being different: weird, crazy, bold, and characterized.

One day, I saw a 50-year-old man, his top was a tight body shirt tucked into some indescribable trousers. I really don't know how to describe it. So… it was like this: the bottom was bell shaped as much as it could, then it molded his thigh up to the belly. From behind, it looked like he shook his bottom to left and right, but in front it was a fashion disaster. Because in front, it worked same way as lady's legging. So... you got what I meant huh? The effect seemed to bam into the eyes of viewers as if there was an unbalance "thing" right there in the middle but a bit out of the way. If he were in Vietnam, he would be featured on Kenh14.vn, Zing.vn or Vnexpress.net[9] for sure. Or an old lady who was in a sexy lace top, or another one tried shirt cover-up[10] style. Then a young guy with lace jacket outside a tiny cover inside just enough to hide his nipples. They looked weird, strange, and a bit...odd.

But they didn't care. Nobody cared, I was the only one who gave them an admiring strange look, all other passengers just acted like it was normal: not a furtive glance, not pointing at, no comments, no laugh, no camera – you may be sued if you take photos of people.

Thuy – my friend – said, in Japan, people's privacy was protected. If a guy chased a girl but she didn't want it, the guy should not be around her house. She would call the police. Taking photos of people without their permission was not allowed. Yes, it was forbidden. But more than that law was in their self-awareness. When those forbidden things became an awareness, and entered daily life naturally, it might became common sense, and that was another level of civilization.

My friends used to say: "Japanese are naughty". If googling, would find thousands of JAV online. Yes, it was another wild world in Kabukicho playing all night long which could make all red-light

---

9   Big websites for news in Vietnam.

10   Shirt cover-up: long shirt that cover the short which make it look like there is no short.

streets all over the world hat-off. But, kindly let you know, that was not all. Stepping out of Kabukicho, there was a completely different world. You could not find a sex toy store outside of Kabukicho. You can't find any house of prostitution outside of Kabukicho. All sexual activities happened in just that area. Outside of it was the world of wealth, order, well organization, prosperous mixed well with tradition, in a magical way.

It is an advanced country where their people are encouraged to be a free individual. Japanese themselves are citizens of an advanced country, but the good thing is they still preserve the root of their nation. They still respect their national sport – Sumo, temples are still maintained in a very careful and respectful way, social norms are still being upheld and developed to a whole new level. They freely choose their fashion based on their likes, their characteristics within the modest Eastern cultural framework, they can say whatever they like but softly, gently, and humbly. There is nothing forced here. It is like every baby girl in Vietnam would have to learn by heart the rule that if they go out alone they would be kidnapped and raped, when mom is not home, if they open doors to strangers, they would be cheated, their house would be robbed, they should never trust a stranger. The basic lesson would follow them until when they grow up, the point is just what their lesson is?

Or, another story when I went to restaurant. A waiter kneeled down to write the order. I stood up immediately because I couldn't do that, I could not sit still acting like I was a customer. Japanese was strange. The waiter looked at me and smile. He said it was ok, it was normal. It was not once but whatever restaurant I entered, they would treat their customers that way. After the first time I stood up in surprise, I started to watch the surroundings and got used to such custom. That was the service. And talking about service, nowhere would beat Japan. From street food vendors to luxury restaurants, from shopping malls to convenient stores, you would always see smiles of the shopkeeper lady, of the waiter who just passed by to ask if you needed anything else. Many times, I thought when I write something about Japan, I should input some negative comments to balance my viewpoint. But, really, I didn't find anything to complain. I just can say everything is at perfect level. But there is nothing perfect in this world? Just come to Japan, to finish your doubt, to open your heart and to trust in human. Perfection is the value that a society offers to people who live in it. And I once posted on my Facebook: If you ever fall in love, fall with a Japanese.

There were couples of times I almost died of heartache for not being able to find a toilet while walking around Los Angeles downtown. Over there, shops didn't have their own toilet, even if they have, they would lock it with password and only their staff can open to customers. While in Tokyo, and other Japanese cities, toilets are freely open. Whenever you feel need to, for sure there would be guidance showing you the way to the nearest restrooms right in front of you. Public toilets in every city always haunt me for being super dirty, and people give a sh** about common hygiene. Yet, in Japan, they were perfect to my surprise. No matter what size, no matter where, subway station, airport or on the street, they all were astonishingly clean and clear. They were equipped with state-of-the-art technology, not a single water-drop left, washing system was with warm water and water gun, and they smelled really good. Perfect! There seemed to be no difference between 5-star toilet and on-the-street toilet. If talking about value they offer, users receive the same value from both. Everything is convenient and clean. This is enhanced to become a public awareness. See, that is how strange they are.

Of course, you would not see any worker standing in the toilet watching the whole thing and his hand holding a mop. Labor rate in Japan is really high, hiring someone just to do so would not be popular. They reach that kind of hygiene level thanks to the collective awareness. Only common sense of hygiene, of respecting other people, respecting the community that we belong to, together aiming at a communal value not the petty individual interest can create such. I was not surprised while walking on the street and saw someone picking up garbage to throw into the bin. Oh, by the way, even the garbage separation system in Japan was complicated, more than USA and Europe, including garbage of plastic, glass, paper, plastic box and other, etc. Customers of McDonalds, Starbucks, and fast food places carefully separated garbage after finishing their meals and then returned the trays to the correct location. They made me – a stranger customer from a country where we got too used to being fully served from the moment we walked in until when we walked out – feel like I was an useless person because we can't do just that simple thing while in Vietnam. That is why, after this, who goes to coffee shops with me would know my habit that I would clean everything before I leave. I believe that if everybody together does that, we can save a lot labor and money. And more importantly, to improve common sense which is seriously lack of in my country.

Due to the high cost of labor, I was surprised once I went eat out with a Japanese customer. That day, I would have dinner with Mr. Ken Samizo. He was a customer of my company in Vietnam, he visited a couple of times and I was the one who welcomed him. Therefore, when I went to Tokyo, I texted him. A late afternoon, he came to my hostel to bring me to a sushi place near there. After sitting at the table, I looked around to find some staff. Before I could ask Mr. Ken, I heard a hello coming from the tablet on the table. He picked it up, clicked on menu and asked what I wanted. I asked him, "We order by this?" "Yes". He then pressed on dishes and "Enter" without forgetting two tasty Japanese beers. Not long after, the food came. All was so quick that I couldn't imagine. I thought about sushi places where staff were more than customers and laughed. Ken got why I laughed, and he also smiled. We had a lot of laugh in that dinner because there were so many new things that I discovered and was amazed.

Previous time when he went to Vietnam, he insisted on finding a Japanese interpreter. I didn't get it because he wrote email in a pretty good English. I asked him some questions while on taxi, but he just shortly answered and then nothing more. I thought, was Japanese arrogant? Or they didn't appreciate Vietnamese? And then all our communication between us had been via the interpreter. If we didn't meet in person but just worked via email, everything was smooth. This time, we did not have any interpreter. I sat in front of him in the famous sushi Hokkaido. I tried to talk slowly in English. Some sentences he could understand, some he didn't. but smiled. Then he mixed between English and Japanese that confused me. Then he explained to me the reason behind the things I hadn't understand: He used Google Translate. He typed in Japanese, had it translated and showed me. I replied by typing English for translation and showed him. Oh my, so he had been using Google Translate for the whole time. If it was true, I must give Google an applause. Because it did a great job, very good translation. But the dearest thing was the way Ken apologized. He felt sorry for not being able to communicate with me. He kept saying sorry, tried to explain though the more he explained the more Japanese he used. The meal went well in laughter of understanding though not much communication. And I knew that I already passed the basic level of communication which was language to better understand each other. We used to feel hesitated if thinking of travelling to a place where people don't speak English. It's of course, right? But once we face it, I believe that even when we don't speak human language, we still can find way to make ourselves understood, that is using the language of universe: body language. It helps people overcome challenges to go further, to places where they used to think they "can't". Yes, nothing is impossible. Only dare or not? Right?

Nothing was so bad that something good could not come from it. Due to not much communication, we focused on eating. Being a visitor, I was treated with many fine dishes of Japanese. I ate slowly, this and that. Food like fresh octopus, fresh shrimps, etc. maybe I would not be able to pay for them in Vietnam. Now, they were there for me to enjoy. However, the most impressive one was Hokkaido crab's nippers. With this kind of crab, you can only eat their nippers, and they only can survive in Hokkaido, that was why it was specialty. Crab's meat was awesome. To a person who loves to eat like me, it was the best sea food I had ever had. Last time when Ken visited Vietnam, I had treated him a dinner in Ngoc Suong Marina[11] so this time he treated me the same. I was budget travelling, did not have money for such. But as old people said: the more you give, the more you get. Ken also said:

- Don't worry, while in Japan, no one would take your money if they do nothing for you.

It was Sunday evening, at 8pm… I sighed with relief, walked on barefoot into the elevator up to 6th floor, threw myself on the cold capsule bed. I felt safe mentally, but to be honest, I didn't know what to do. I decided that maybe I would climb Fuji mountain on Monday morning. I tried online booking for a mountain tour, but then received an auto-reply: We need at least 24 hours to proceed your request. That means they hadn't confirmed my booking because it was Sunday evening. I ran down to the reception, asking how to deal with this. They advised me that just go to the bus station tomorrow morning. Ok, just go there tomorrow. Eventually, I had

---

11   An expensive restaurant chain in Vietnam

no idea what to do. The price for that tour was more than 400USD!!! Couldn't lose it.

About 10 pm, I received email from the agency saying they did not have enough time to arrange my booking and asked if I wanted to change date or cancel the booking. I didn't have much time left for Tokyo, there was no other way but to cancel it. They agreed and would release the money they voided from my credit card. As a backpacker, paying 400 USD to climb mountain was too much. But I tried taking the chance, knowing that opportunity was not always available. However, I was refunded that 400 USD, it was good already, so I had a good sleep. Before deeply falling into sleep, I thought about all things and really admired the way of service that Japanese offered their customers. They were honest, from the inside and as a system.

And because they were a system of honesty, I realized I had nothing to worry about here. I did not trust any city where I had visited as much as I trusted Japanese cities. I trust them absolutely. Trust was not luxury here, it was overwhelmed from the inside of people I met, from their acts of kindness. Don't think I exaggerated. I truly experienced such. Everybody says, "Doing business with Japanese is the safest". They are serious, faithful, safe, clear, and reliable. Even an employee in Japan may not need contract. Between them are rules: rules of dedication, no changing jobs, no unhealthy competition, not trying to win competitor's employee. Between them is the mutual respect for mutual development.

The road in green

I n summer, Gingko trees at both sides of streets were lively colored with green. In Tokyo, gingkoes were planted many, used as divider between vehicle lane and pedestrian lane. In fall, it was like someone accidentally poured a whole can of yellow onto gingko leaves creating one of the most romantic scene. Every day, across those busy streets, there was a guy holding the phone, staring to Google Maps to find direction. To be honest, on first days in Japan, I suffered a lot from the language. Because I could not remember the words, everything was the same to me: road names, stations, people's name, foods, etc. Everything sounded same to me, confusingly. But after some days in Tokyo with countless times of getting on and off the subway, walking through countless streets, reading maps like every second, things seemed to be better and familiar. From the hostel, walking out, turning left a bit would be the biggest shopping mall in Tokyo – Isetan. Below Isetan was Shinjuku-Sanchome subway station, that was where I would start my daily discovery. There would be a Starbucks on 1st Floor which was full of customers at any time in the day, a huge H&M, a multistory Zara and a ramen place with free but slow Wi-Fi, etc.

Previously, when I purchased my MacBook, the seller had saved many high-quality photos of Japan (copyright by Apple, of course). I set one of it as wallpaper – it was a Tokyo from above. That photo rooted into my mind the intention that "I must climb up high to get this view". There were two ways to see Tokyo from above; one was from Tokyo Tower and the other was from Tokyo Metropolitan building. The first way would cost money, much money. So, I chose the other way. In the morning of the date leaving Tokyo, I dragged my stuff to Tokyo Metropolitan Building. Tokyo from the above was beautiful, peaceful and misty as if it were still sleeping. Shinjuku Gyoen National Garden – the lung of the city – impressed the sight with its dark green colour, surrounded by high buildings rising up over low rise houses. If standing from this height, it was impossible to imagine that the under the layer of mist was a busy crowded Tokyo. I got a table by the glass window in the restaurant at 45th Floor for the lunch. It was like there were only me and a Tokyo out there breathing peacefully.

A little bit later after noon, the sun spread its golden shine, but it was not as hot as in Sai Gon. Tokyo temperature at that time was about 5-6 degree less than Saigon. You just needed to sit down under the shadow of a tree, it would be cool and pleasant, even a bit chill if there were many trees.

I sat down on a bench in the big city, closed my eyes, listened to busy steps around. Tokyo was crowded but quiet in a strange way. There was not even a noise. I would take a bus to another city. I tried to imagine if after leaving here, when I close my eyes, what would I recall? Maybe would be my cautious steps first days I was here, would be late nights on empty streets, would be deep bows, would be moments when I lied in the park to hear sounds of birds and playing kids, would be sounds of humble voices, etc. All mixed well in a way that I just wanted to keep in my heart and wrap by peace. The moment when the girl sitting in next bench helped to take a photo of me, a gentle breeze blew by... and moved me.

I came back to that location once again that late afternoon to watch the sunset. The sun poured down its orange colour onto a corner of the city. Tokyo was seeing me off in a dreamy sundown. I quietly enjoyed the gift until the shine completely went off then dragged my stuff to the bus station. Just a bit later, I would travel through the darkness of night to be with a tranquil Kyoto.

KYOTO

Letters for Kyoto

(written in a McDonald's at Kyoto Station)

The night bus made me exhausted. The coldness already soaked into my body, making me awake the whole night while other passengers were sleeping tight as if they were in their own room.

It was 8:42 am here and still not yet 7:00 am in Sai Gon. My friends would be still sleeping. I finished a baguette with sausage and finished my morning coffee in McDonalds, to recharge. I didn't know, there were moments when I felt like my body was drained. Two days ago, when I walked out from a bath in a public bath house, I hardly breathed. I felt like I could get fainted on the tiled floor. Was it because the water was too hot and I dipped myself for too long? I didn't like hot water but wanted to see how long I could handle. Until when I reeled forward out and panted, I realized I did it too much. Sometimes, should not do such crazy thing.

Days before Kyoto, it was like I had worked out intensively: carried nearly ten kilograms on shoulder from 10am to 9pm (nearly

12 hours per day?) to walk around. Leave and back, leave and back, like a diligent commuter. I walked to all roads in Tokyo, too much that painful was not enough to describe. It changed from pain to nothing. My legs? where are they?

I always feel moved when recalling these days. I pity my tiny dwarf body while walking on streets. People sometimes ask why I usually walk with my head down, I don't know. That way of walking really looks pathetic, and sad. But it's ok, despite my head down, I still proudly walk around many strangers who are physically taller than me. Head down is not responsible for how far and how fast we can go. But well, maybe i would change. Yeah... a change...

I love days in Tokyo a lot. But Tokyo was too busy, I myself was also busy and heavy (nine kilograms on shoulders for nearly 12hours/ days, well, tell me it was nothing? You dare?). That was why in Kyoto, I hoped it would be easy.

In Kyoto, there were temples and the legendary bamboo forest. Anything else? I didn't know, and I didn't care. If fate allowed it, I would find it. Just like previous trips. I wanted to immerse myself into the city, to navigate streets and transportation, to get lost among its small alleys first. Plans for places to go and what to do would be later. I wanted that, after every city, I could master it. So that I could tell my friends my stories and inspire them by the feeling I felt in my way.

Japanese, they are strange people. I admired from the old man, to the beautiful girl on street, from the warm-hearted lady to the policeman at the junction. They did not fake, they did not act. They were all polite, tidy, kind, nice, understanding, sympathetic, humble and moderate. Anything other adjectives to describe Japanese? Of all cities I've ever been to, Tokyo was the one I felt secured the most. And now, here I was, in Kyoto – the city of the legendary bamboo forest.

To the ancient capital

When the bus stopped at Kyoto station, it was still cold in the morning. It was summer end, the city got less rain, the sky was high and wide. Other passengers already left. They knew where they would go. But not me. I had no idea where I would go. It was still too early to check in, no need to rush. I dragged my case into Kyoto station, found a McDonald's to fill my stomach. And more importantly, I needed coffee.

It was just early morning but there were many people already. Office men and women in their suits were quietly having their breakfast. They were eating while staring at their phones. Then they finished quickly and cleaned the place and disappeared into the crowd. I was the only one who sat there, slowly ate, slowly used the phone to see what I was gonna do. One thing after one thing, no need to rush. I was leisurely living, slowly feeling... these couldn't be rush...

Before going to Kyoto, I already prepared to live an easy life while in this country. Kyoto was the ancient capital before it was moved to Tokyo with more than 3,000 pagodas and temples. Kyoto nowadays still remained the same, it still had their uniqueness from the past. I read somewhere that in WWII, USA did consider dropping an atomic bomb to Kyoto. But because it was too beautiful, and they wanted to preserve it, they chose the alternatives (which were Nagasaki and Hiroshima). Kyoto saved itself by its beauty. Thank Kyoto, for still being here, for us to see your charms.

I stayed a bit long in the station, for the Wi-Fi. I needed to find places to go today, like stations, bus, hotels. In Japan, Wi-Fi was free at every station. Of course, only for basic needs like: Google Maps, emails, checking information, etc. No Facebook, no Instagram to post selfies. Anyway, if I really wanted to, I just needed to be in McDonald's or 7Eleven. This country was fully equipped. However, Japan was quite inflexible with rules. For example, hotels. They fixed check-in and checkout time, and no exception. I would not be able to do early check-in. Therefore, let do some sightseeing first.

I checked the map the last time, got on the metro to Arashiyama district where there were many pagodas and the Sagano bamboo forest. A girl on the train kindly showed me the station I should got off. She was so kind that I felt a bit sorry. But thanks to days in Tokyo, I was familiar with the cute way that Japanese treated people. I did a deep bow to thank her – the way they would behave.

On the green grassland in Arashiyama

Walking out of the station, looking at people walking toward a small road, I knew where I should go. The map showed that there were many beautiful temples in this area, there were also

Sagano bamboo forest, Hozu river with the bridge Togetsukyo which spanned over the mirror-like water surface, and the hill where you could have a panorama view of the Kyoto. The area was not too big, but merely walking would be a problem. Luckily, I saw a shop where they had bicycles for rent. Luck was the word I used a lot during travelling days. Because if it was not luck, I didn't know what else to call. Two hundred thousand for a bike in one day. Couldn't be better. Vietnamese on a bicycle, c'mon, there would be nothing that could be more reasonable. And with a bike, nothing could stop me from exploring Kyoto. Here I came…

Arashiyama in summer end was as green as a carpet in the middle of the high wide sky. I just wanted to cycle straight to the bamboo forest. In every travel guides, Sagano bamboo forest was on the list of mustvisit places must visit before died. It was.

It was a big area full of bamboo. The green, vertical bamboo intertwined to each other creating a spectacular scenery. Even the sound created by the wind going through the forest was one of the sounds that needed to be preserved by the Japanese. Stepping in here, I felt like travelling back to a dynasty of some centuries ago. The mark of modern world seemed not to exist. Even when arriving unpopulated areas, I could even imagine a few Ninja hiding in the deep green forest. When I arrived at the most beautiful area, it was packed with many people. Tourists using selfie sticks crazily taking photos, students in neat uniforms standing align, rickshaws waiting for guests, groups speaking a language that anyone could identify where they were from. Looking at tourists sweating a lot due to walking, I felt myself genius for renting a bike. I didn't forget to ask for help from a Korean girl to take a photo of me. She was really dedicated, asking me to change poses.

Along the roads filled with fresh air and the cool green colour, I cycled to famous ancient temples in West North of Kyoto. Japanese temples were places of absolute quietness. You may feel rude and embarrassed if you walk too strong. Especially, temples in Kyoto were usually surrounded by vast greenery. Besides, there were flowers, wellsprings, Zen gardens, tea houses, etc. All together created an irresistibly poetic scene. The green mosses of time made me linger. There were many maple trees in this area. No doubt that during autumn, this place would be painted with orange red colour. It was the specialty of Kyoto in Autumn. I would go there once, once possible.

Let's live days of worry-free

Leaving Ashimaya, I went back to the city center by metro. I didn't see any ticket machine. I was a bit worried that if I didn't have ticket, I would be fined. I didn't want to discredit Vietnamese. So, I asked a young lady who was holding a baby. She then quickly stood up, walked around to read bulletins in Japanese then backed and shook her head. I was like "Huh?" What did that mean? She didn't speak English but kept on speaking Japanese, I didn't understand anything. After 10 minutes trying to use body language, she asked the person sitting next to her to help interpret. So, the matter was, they didn't sell ticket at this station, until the terminal. The train arrived just in time after I understood the issue.

This seemed to be the oldest train in Japan, even its passengers were all the oldies. The train ran fast and its wheels grinded against the rail. The train looked so old that it made me worried, would it run into houses on both sides? Luckily, it was just my coward fear, nothing happened?

I bravely walked into the hotel. The receptionist asked me: how many nights? I showed him a super nice smile: two nights. He checked and said: you only stay tonight. I was like "What?" My smile immediately disappeared.

Oh my Gosh. So, the night before leaving for Kyoto, not sure if I were sleepy then, I booked for two nights while one of them was the night I slept on the bus. That meant I paid for one night I didn't stay!?! I then hoped that the receptionist would feel pity for me because Japanese always tried to help. So, I smiled with him again and started to tell him my story. I beg him for sympathy because I had been confused, I booked for wrong date, and asked him if I could change? Well, I forgot that, not only being kind, Japanese were also famous for being inflexible. And this time, their inflexibility worked: a NO from the receptionist. Anyway, still had to pay, checked in.

After got into the room, I tried to email Agoda to negotiate, and the answer again was "rules are rules". I lost 1.2 million VND. It hurt! I was not angry with them, I was angry with me actually. This kind of thing happened once before. One time, I bought air ticket.

The departing flight was ok, but until when I went to the airport to fly back, that I knew I should have flown two days before that. What a shame of me, huh?

I stayed at Ark Hotel Kyoto. After days staying in the capsule hostel in Tokyo, I thought it was not necessary to try that model any more. I needed a private space for good sleep, not shared space with a bunch of people getting in and out talking blah blah blah the whole day preventing me from deep sleep. And I didn't want to share bathroom with naked people around. I chose this hotel because it was right in the center of Kyoto, near Nijo castle, Kyoto ocean park and Nishiki market. Kawaramachi and Kyoto Imperial Palace were near there too.

From the hotel, I could easily access visiting sites by walk or by bicycle.

Those days were my peaceful days. I woke up in the morning and realized I was in Tokyo, then slowly walked a bit to the place where they had the super good udon at the next junction. In the afternoon, I would cycle to other sites or maybe just cycle around exploring the city or dropped by the Starbucks which was celebrating their 15th anniversary being in Kyoto. In the evening, I wandered in Nishiki market choosing cute handicraft items, or went to a takoyaki place to eat my favourite place. It was the place where in front they had a fake octopus made by transparent plastic. If I was still hungry late at night, I could across the street to the McDonald's opposite to enjoy the supper.

If someone asked me "How was your day, anything special?" I would say No. That is just the way I choose to enjoy strange city. Just enjoy the life the way a local would enjoy, live the day as peaceful as possible. So that when we leave it, everything of the city, even the smell of the breeze becomes an unspeakable nostalgia. In Vietnam we have a famous poem which I think best fits:

"When I'm there, it is just a place.

When I leave, it becomes my soul."

OSAKA
NIGHT OF VIETNAMESE CULTURE

———

Japan people

I woke up the other day, checked out the hotel (again), jumped on a bus to head Kyoto station. The bus was full of people, but everyone always made way for me because I was with my luggage. I apologized but everybody smiled and said it was ok. I was not really happy when knowing the fact that this kindness would not happen in my Sai Gon. People were easy to get annoyed.

Japan was country of automation with the best robotic manufacture in the world, therefore small things such as ticketing would not need human labor, they mainly had machines to take care of this. There were many ways to go from Kyoto to Osaka, but I wanted to go by train. The thing that made me hesitated was choosing between cheap train or Shinkansen high-speed train. The difference of prices was 200,000 (100,000 for normal train and 300,000 for high-speed train). I already experienced the feeling of travelling with high-speed train while in Europe, but I was a fun-loving person, so I still wanted to try. Ok, 300 thousand, here we go!

After dragging my stuff to the platform, I stood in line just like everyone else. I asked the person standing in front: "Is it Shinkansen?" He said "No, this is normal train". I asked, "So how to get Shinkansen?" Just then, the train arrived. The man stepped out of the line and grabbed my hand leading me. I said, "I can find it my own, just get on your train, otherwise you will be late". He said: "It's ok, let me help you".

That was a Japanese.

Not a specific individual but it was the figure of the whole society. Imagine this, I spoke zero Japanese, I was there alone, every day I walked around streets, trains, shopping malls, temples, etc. then what helped me out of trouble? It was those kind people around who always offered their help, always smiled when I asked them and always welcomed when I said I was from Vietnam. In their eyes, I could see that they liked Vietnam people. Maybe because of the way Vietnamese helped Japanese when they came to our country. Also, funny thing, if I said, "I'm from Vietnam" then 100% the reply would be "I've been there, Ha Long Bay is really beautiful." Or "I would go there soon." This kind of friendliness and closeness was kinda rare in Asia. Therefore, if you travel to Japan without speaking their language, even solo or in group, don't be nervous, just go, nothing difficult over there. Because it is Japan.

On the train, when I was intently writing, the passenger next to me reminded: Arriving Shin-Osaka! I was like "what?" I just got on, found my seat, then took out iPad and just some lines only. Arrive already? Really? The train was too fast, or I was too slow? I hadn't felt anything called high-speed, damn, I wasted 400 thousand :(the only thing I could felt was like I missed step when going along the aisle finding my seat while the train was running. The landscape outside the window passed by very, very fast. I didn't enjoy anything...

Seemed like I was never able to write anything about a city during the time I was there. Between real-time writing and recall writing, I choose the latter. That means after each trip, I would just let my mind calm down for about one week, two weeks, one month or even one year (e.g. the trip to Luang Pra Bang). Things remain after that would be the most impressive. And once I write, the flow of feeling just pours out until the final period. Nothing is forced, nothing can distract. Sometimes, when I really want to write about some place, I still can try my best to come up with some words. Of course, they would be deleted right after that. Only when I am satisfied with what I wrote, then so do my friends, I believe so. Before, now and later, I would always be a carefree writer. The carefreeness is to ensure the purity, and the truthfulness of the story and also, I don't want to change myself.

For many reasons, Osaka was a city which took me like forever to start writing about it. Honestly, after confusing days in crowded Tokyo, and Japanese tasteful days in Kyoto, I came to Osaka with a different purpose. I was to find the modern taste of a city. And the characteristics of modern cities seemed to be the same everywhere: high rise buildings, huge shopping malls, multi-lane highways. For sure I would spend time shopping and doing some "modern" stuff.

Quy texted: "Oh, poor you, you've gotta spend a lot of money in Osaka."

Well, yeah, I did. Because my body was a bit like Japanese size, small and slim. I kept on blinding myself "I won't have another chance. Buy good things. Japanese goods are famous for their quality". Most of the trip was just shopping and shopping, that was why I had nothing to write about.

Yet, there was one thing I found in Osaka by chance that made me really, really happy.

Fellowmen

Not sure if Japan was too big, people were too many or I was too small, but during the whole week in Tokyo, Kyoto and now Osaka, I had never heard a single Vietnamese. Bro Cuong from Australia had asked if I needed any help, or someone to show me around because he had a Vietnamese friend living in Japan with his family. I said no need, I could handle it. In trips that I decided to go alone, I didn't feel like communicating with fellow men. I prefer a local, to learn about their culture, their people, their food, and get some tips. If no one, then should be alone.

The afternoon in Osaka castle, while sitting mindlessly on the bench looking at the birds playing on the yard, I suddenly overheard a familiar language: Vietnamese. Not sure why but I felt really happy then. They were a group of Vietnamese tourists. Families were travelling together, laughing with each other. I sat there, quietly looked at them, while inside I was thrilled by happiness. It had been one week already, I hadn't heard or spoken any single word of this beloved language. I missed it. The intensity of how much I missed it wanted to drag me to come and talk to them, to tell them I was a Vietnamese too. But the inherent character stopped me, I still sat there watching them. They were travelling by tours.

I don't know if anyone of you has ever experienced this: your hearing and speaking abilities are still fine, but for a time under some situation, you don't speak or hear any word of your mother tongue. You are exposed continuously to a strange language which you don't understand even a single word, so much that your feeling won't work the same way it used to work. That was me after one week no Vietnamese. Until that moment, I realized how much I loved my language. The need to speak was like the need to eat, to drink, to sleep and to be loved. I had always been in my own environment, so much that I forgot how dear it was. Therefore, in an afternoon in a strange city of a foreign country, I was moved. The emotion that had been repressed for days created a spring waiting to burst open. I stood up, followed them...

When we reached the highest watch tower of the castle, I asked a lady who was travelling with a 17-year-old son to take a photo of me.

I spoke in Vietnamese: "Dạ cô chụp giúp con tấm hình nhé?" (Ms., could you please help take a photo of me?).

She smiled and said: "Ừ, để cô." (Let me).

After taking photo, she asked: "Con đi đoàn nào?" (Which group are you?)

I replied: "Dạ không, con đi một mình" (No, I am alone)

144

She was surprised: "Ủa con tự đi đó hả?" (What, you self-arranged your trip?)

Her son jumped in before I managed to answer: "Không thể. Sao anh đi một mình được. Em nghe nói xin visa khó lắm, mà anh biết tiếng Nhật không?" (Impossible. How can you go alone? I heard that visa was so difficult. But can you speak Japanese?)

I shook my head: Nope

He continued: "I haven't met anyone speaking English, how can you go alone?"

I told you: "Why not? Here I am!"

Yes, here I was, in Osaka. I said goodbye to them and left. To be honest, I hoped that one day, the son would grow up and less suspect of impossibilities. There is no limit in this life, as well no standard. You just need to believe, then you can do it.

When the hunger of Vietnamese as well as fish sauce reached the peak, luck smiled at me again. That night, I met two girls: Linh and Thuy. Linh was a young friend, used to work with me in HSBC. She was now in Osaka working for a bank. Thuy was an interpreter. When three of us got together, we couldn't stop talking. At the beginning, we tried to lower our voices and laughter, but after a while, we couldn't hold it, we laughed out loud. Someone walked by and stared at us, maybe because we were so noisy. But we didn't care, we were Vietnamese. And I believe among those who saw us, there would be some thought that we were fighting. Well, living quietly and softly was not always good, haha.

Night of Vietnamese culture

L inh texted: Bro, party tonight.

I won't deny it, I love bar and pub and beer and cocktails. I always try to go to famous bars whenever I travel to a city. To see what music they play, what dance they like, what drinks they have. To see how their youth dresses, how they shout, how the prices. Good ideas huh? But, indeed, I just walk in there, sit at the bar, order a mojito, order another one. I enjoy the feeling of merging myself with the music, with the noise and smiling eyes. Suddenly I recalled the moment I was impressed to freeze when seeing people did Apsara dance in a bar name "The heart of darkness" in Phnom Penh, Cambodia. In Japan should be different, huh?

I agreed immediately. Clubbing in Osaka, why wait?

By nightfall, Osaka was shining with sparkling lights. The culture of neon signs in Japan made everything become unusually fascinating. Linh and Thuy turned up, more beautiful than normal. We dropped by a familiar Japanese place for sushi, enjoyed the notorious dry fried fish. The day before, we ordered one for three, everyone had wanted more. Now, we were generous, three for three. Eyes were bigger than mouths. After the fish, we couldn't finish the rest. Whatever, it was weekend. Live a worthy life.

Leaving Umeda, we got on subway to Namba. If anyone ever visited Osaka, you would be familiar with this famous Namba area. It was called the area for the youth. Endless fashion shops, restaurants, karaoke, wine places, thrift shops, all in the race of signs. Thuy laughed and asked: "So where are we going?" "Why, you are the one who knows the best".

So, because it was still early, we decided to watch movie. The time would be perfect then for clubbing. It took us a while to discuss which movie. I wanted to watch the Japanese ghost movie that had just been released couple days ago. (Well, for sure I just could watch the graphic, forget the audio part, I wouldn't understand anyway.) Linh and Thuy wanted to watch an American movie. We finally agreed on "Need for speech", action movie and seemed to be understandable. The first time I went watch movie in Japan, I was again impressed by how much automatic Japan was. Buying tickets -> vending machine. Popcorn and drinks -> vending machine. Find the screen, find the seat, watch, leave, and tidy up your own place – all by yourself. There were only couples of staff at information counter, they answered questions if any. You took care the rest by yourself.

It was an awful movie, I have to say. The cinema was empty, so we joked with each other that we paid for all. It was an English-speaking movie, subtitled in Japanese, so we needed Thuy to interpret if we could not catch up. It was not an easy watching. Thuy was a Ha Noi girl, she came to Japan to study then married to a Japanese. She had been working as an interpreter for a Japanese bank. She could speak Japanese fluently. Even the hotel I was staying in Osaka was a help from her. I could not find such a cheaper hotel from Agoda. I was much more confident if being with her in Japan.

It was 11 pm when we finished the movie. We looked at each other questioning "What now?". Luckily, thanks to what was called

"Backpacking experience", I searched for the keyword "party hard in Namba", it showed a bunch of places. After a tiring walk around the market, we chose Pure to spend the rest of this weekend night.

It was packed. They sat at tables and at the bar. After ordering out drinks, we chose a place to the left of the dance floor. Drank a bit, got high a bit. Now, let's dance!

I am not sure whether Japanese, who are notorious for being shy dance, really knows how to dance? The floor was empty regardless of the rising sound of Girl Gone Wild remix that was playing loudly and could charm anyone. Anyway, we didn't care! We owned the place!

After a while, it became a bit more crowded. A group of four people joined us, one of them was a girl whose mother was Vietnamese. I thought there were Asian-Americans, because they were different. Then it looked like people already felt the beat, more people joined us on the dance floor. There were some still sitting at their table acting "classy" and looking at those crazy "creatures" in the middle of the room. The three Vietnamese of us just kept on dancing, drinking, laughing and having fun. It was an awesome combination of alcohol and music in a place where nobody knew you. Even Thuy and Linh who was living here but never tried checking this out. They were good girls. I had a different point of view, they could be good and enjoy life at the same time. You just need to know the limit and don't cross it.

That night, Linh was the one who shone. Many Japanese young guys, tall and handsome in business suits came to ask her for a dance. Although she was not the most beautiful with the best body. What made her different? Maybe the friendliness and freedom. Those Japanese girls just stood there in their bubbles, looking at people with shyness. Linh and Thuy were not like that. Because we didn't care what people think about us. We danced the most popular and crazy dances, from the Boom Boom POW to Apsara, from Vietnamese traditional to even one-leg hopping connecting people. Nothing bad. C'mon, who care? All eyes were staring at us – the crazy dancers who actually couldn't dance. But we were happy, joyful, energetic, and friendly. There were more and more people joining and making friends with us, which made us kinda embarrassed. So we left. It was enough for Japanese to see how Vietnamese partied. We called it "A Vietnamese culture promotion event".

It was 2:30 am when we left, and the night did not really finish. We didn't want to go home yet. We chose to end the night by just strolling around, on Osaka quiet streets at night. We walked and talked, no one wanted to mention that "hey, it's time to go home".

You know, sometimes, those are the best moments ever to spend with friends, just walking around, talking, sitting down on a bench or even on pavement with endless stories…

Until 4:00 am, we decided to say goodbye. Linh and Thuy took a taxi, and I was on another one. It was already dawn by the time I arrived the hotel.

Osaka, those were the days, days of being young, at heart…

CHAPTER 8

BHUTAN

D id I say... that I would fly to Bhutan this weekend? Goodbye the old year, hello the new year – at same place.

This year has been quite special to me, it is totally for experience. I quit job after the Europe trip early in the year, then I quickly found myself on a night flight to Canada. Soon after that, I already wrapped myself in scarves walking on the way to the University of Ottawa.

In the gorgeous yard of that old-established school, I stood still for how long I didn't know. What I wanted to say? I did not either know. Maybe just... "Hi, it's late... but I'm here".

After enjoying the sea in Cuba and stopping by the US to visit some friends, I backed to Vietnam in September, travelled a bit and then decided not to work for any company yet but focusing on finding fund for my own business. Wrap up the year with resolutions of new year!

The biggest lesson of this year would just be encapsulated in a brief line: If I can lift it up, I can let it go. I quitted a good job, left a great position just to hop on the Bus 12 every day to school. I became more drastic with my own personality: be more straightforward, more honest and more real. I separated myself from the majority, to see the simplest things.

Together with that, I nourish my life with experience. Money in then out, people love then leave. But experience will still be there, forever, more and more over time.

Did I say… that I would fly to Bhutan this weekend? Wrap up a fulfilling year, and await wonderful days of new year.

THE MAGNIFICENT SMOKY SKY

I woke up early one morning, and took that opportunity to walk to the village. This time, most were still wrapping themselves in blankets. It was cold outside, too cold at minus four degrees. With the travelling agenda this time which I hardly found any alone time like previous trips, with my personalities, I'd better make use of the time being here. In Bhutan, it is impossible, or to say in another world, no one does that – no one gallivants in village to take photos or freely books a room in downtown. Maybe I was one of a few who did such, this time a little bit and would be a bit more next times. I said to the tour guide that I would come back, would stay longer and wander more, until when I can memorize every corner, every street and every kind face I met.

What else about Bhutan? I don't know! If there is anything special that exists nowhere in the world but here, it must be the energy of peace. The peace of a country who is noiseless to the world though down there at the foot of the Himalayas lies a raging river. Neither Pho Chu nor Mo Chu, I am not talking about those holy rivers. I am talking about another one, the one of life out there where it is noisy and people are trapped in corners created by themselves.

Whilst here, standing on the slope looking down to the river of positive energy, the river is stronger than any other rivers in the world but still as smooth as an early morning with silk hanging over the sky.

One afternoon, when the check-in had been completed, I decided to walk around Naksel hotel whose precinct was as beautiful as any picture. Smoke rising from houses' chimneys serenely soaked up the beautiful sunlight. It had been long since I saw this. People had changed to using gas or electronic stoves long time ago already. I missed family meals at sunsets, warm kettles in freezing days, etc. I missed those cozy feelings. Kids were playing bows and arrows and laughing happily. It was still cold. On the other side, the Himalayas was hiding the sun, making its way into the darkness. Though being called hotel, Naksel was designed with traditional style, in harmony with nature. Therefore, it gave me the feeling of wandering in a garden at halfway up the mountain. I now could see my breath…

That was it: smokes. I would come back with the first story – the story of a morning walking in a village. I saw an old man spinning prayer wheel and whispering chanting. The image was so beautiful in a new year's morning. I stood by the fence and made a bow. He replied my hello, still reading his chanting and stepping around the wheel. I motioned asking if I could open the gate to come in. He smiled to welcome. That was it. He and I walked for a very long time around the big praying wheel located in his yard. I am quite sure that he did that every morning. That was how Bhutanese start their day, going to temples or rotating the praying wheel at home. The fire outside almost burned down, its smoke curled upwards to the canopy.

Two strangers just kept on walking and walking. There were times when language was surplus. I could feel there was something running inside of me, strong but deep, wild but peace.

While writing these lines, I was listening a strange album: Music of Bhutan – a collection of songs with chanting, flute and sounds of mountains. It evoked many memories. It recalled the night when everybody wore National Dress of Bhutan, danced and drank tea – there are moments that we don't want them to end, as if I had stepped out of that house, the cold wind would have blown me away. While everybody was still thanking and blessing each other, I walked out, respectfully stood in front of Buddha statue and looked at the moon. I just prayed for my mind to become bright, to see and to comprehend. And the most importance was: to see myself.

Then I think of Bhutan as a huge mirror hanging among pine tree lines – the mirror to see ourselves. Being with peaceable people, we become ugly with thoughts, with subsistence and with greed-ignoranceanger. I can't become them, waking up every morning offering clean water with pure worship. I just can hope become a better me – looking at me in that mirror, to correct myself, to let things go, and to accept. Once accepting self, faith would come naturally, and unshakeable.

Last days in Bhutan, I couldn't handle any piece of meat. That is one thing I love a lot about Bhutan. When bowls of white rice were served with a bit of vegetables, they already could make me happy. Purified – not only by the chanting in Paro Taktsang Monastery. Our body has absorbed way too much unclean stuff, it needs cleansing.

Even the air in Bhutan is unwailful, and bloodless; they don't kill any animals. Until being here, I had not believed that there would be any place in the world where people could still keep their purity like this.

And the pure mind of Bhutan people is kind of like a wisp of smoke, as thin as silk, flying up high in the twilight. Thin but gorgeous, as if thousands or millions of years have passed by just in a second, like the first light of sun shining over the Himalayas, like a carefree smile in this scramble world.

* * *

Did I say… that the Bhutan trip that just happened was a trip full of strange things. Like I woke up every morning at 6:00 am to watch the sun rise over the Himalayas. I weirdly got terrified seeing meat in last days of the trip. Or like I walked up to 10 kilometers at the height of 3,000 meters above sea level to get to one of the most sacred places in Bhutan – the Tiger's Nest. You may find it ordinary, but nope, to me, they are not ordinary. To me, they are things that may just happened once in my lifetime.

Did I say… that the trip brought me great friends. They have their own characteristics; we are different but we are compatible. Honestly, in this peaceful place, finding things in common from others is not too difficult. People come here wishing to purify their hearts, to see things they have never seen, and to cultivate their spirits in this thick atmosphere of religious.

Did I say… that one day in Bhutan was equal to many days in other places in the world. The energy received were a lot. In this country, no killing, no smell of blood, every single person is a pure spirit. Is this the world's happiest country? Why people are so nice and kind and warm, smiles are always on their faces and they even made us laugh. During the 5-day journey, I heard no fighting, even a dog would just simply sleep on pavement, ignoring strangers.

And… did I say… that I would come back? I want to return to the place where the sun rise over the highest mountains, smile is the language and kindness is the souvenir to visitors…

CHAPTER 9

TAIPEI TYPHOON

Two days before I flew, I sent 4 requests for couch surfing in Taipei. One was in Japan, one had just been back from the US so he couldn't manage to host me but would hangout and guide me to try local food, one more was in exam but promised to show me around. The last one was Fong. Fong said he had to visit his parents at weekend, but I could stay at his place one night if I wanted.

Right on the first day arriving Taipei, I rushed out until I got exhausted. Imagine, I caught a red-eye flight at 1:30 am whose duration was three and a half hours. Down there was all ocean. My airline – Vietjet[12] – whose seat was too small to sleep on, not to mention it was stormy causing terrible turbulence, every passenger silently looked forward to the landing.

I arrived early in the morning, took bus to the city starting a long journey throughout that whole day. I first started at Floor 89th Taipei101 (the Observatory) to see Taipei at full scale. Taipei101 is the tallest building in Taiwan and the second world tallest building. It

------

12   *Vietjet Air is a Vietnam-based low-cost airline, popularly known as "bikini airline".*

used to be the tallest but now a building in Dubai has already taken its record. Then I went to SOGO to do window shopping, after that was a memorial to a Taiwanese national figure. I spent the rest of energy to hike Elephant mountain for the best view of Taipei one more time – still with the backpack since leaving Vietnam. Fortunately, I met Ethan from the US on the way. Ethan was teaching in Shanghai. We talked about everything under the open sky, making the road felt shorter! But "felt shorter" didn't mean less tired. I breathed in pants like a buffalo, soaked with sweat. It made me realize the days training hard in gym, jogging, climbing and crazy squats – all were beneficial, although I myself don't like these kinds of physical activities. Nevertheless, the hiking trails in Taiwan were quite pleasant. They had options for people to follow. There were rest stops along the way with great view of the city. Even old people and children could do the hike.

Said it was easy, and short, but the way down to the foot, my legs became horrible. Ethan had to go home to get ready for the flight back to Shanghai. The sudden rain forced us to sprint back to the MRT station. And then a brilliant idea came to my mind: to enjoy authentic hot springs in Beitou[13] – to do foot bath and wash away the smell of sweat. I was so exhausted that after more than ten stations, I felt asleep already. It was getting dark. The road to the hot spring was incredibly peaceful. Taipei was surrounded by volcanoes, creating scarcely less famous hot springs than Japanese ones. The hot springs were in the suburb, near the mountains and ran from natural hot water sources to make sure good quality for people.

---

13   Beitou is a northern district, located within Taipei city, famous for its hot springs.

Most days in Taiwan, the word I heard the most was Typhoon. I didn't feel it much except watching weather forecast on TV showing two circles intersect each other. Otherwise, the sun still shone and the days were still warm.

One morning, Fong asked if I wanted to go somewhere. I said I wanted to visit the Taroko Nation Park. Fong said "there is typhoon, I'm afraid it's not appropriate to go there." It was a huge national park, not to mention it took three to four hours by train. To get there and get back in the day may be a bit unmanageable. So I gave up the idea. Fong suggested taking me to Yangmingshan[14] and trying foot bath in natural hot spring heated by volcano. "I have bike", he said. Having chance to experience things that were so local in a strange country was awesome, isn't it?

It was crowded in the hot spring. As regulated, I must wear bath suit, so I bought one and headed to the bath area which had several round pools with various heat levels. The top one was the hottest, running down to lesser hot ones, and thus, people could choose different pools for their best fit.

I looked around, oh my god, all were old people. Did I go to wrong place? Or was this for just old ones? I looked again and now I saw someone young – a group of boys and girls were soaking in the middle of the pool. I was told later by my friend that young people usually went there in mornings, and in the evening, most of guests were the old. Well... I was old anyway.

---

14   Yangmingshan National Park: one of the nine national parks in Taiwan, locating between Taipei and New Taipei City

The weary legs got better after dipping in hot water. However, the pool was too small for too many people. It somehow caused stress. To be honest, there were some seconds I wondered if they boiled the water then poured in the pool. But days after that, I learnt one thing about Taiwanese: they are honest. The water does run from the ground.

Not like Singapore or Hong Kong, the places I don't think I would come back because they are packed and stuffy. But the day I left Taiwan, sitting alone at Taipei Main station, I knew that I must come back. I think within Asia, Taiwan is the only country that can be compared with Japan. The influence of Japan on the whole country was obvious, and inclusive. Each corner was incredibly clean, people seriously queued in line for subway, they talked softly or kept absolutely silent in public. What I had seen in Japan was applied harmoniously in Taiwan But, I can say that apart from the language which is Mandarin – but not really sounds like the main lain Mandarin, there is nothing Chinese on this island. Taiwanese are proud of their small nation. It is understandable. They have many to be proud of. They can buy ticket and fly to USA, Japan and Schengen without visa submission in advance. It is even hard for main lain Chinese to apply for Taiwan visa. They are quite selective about who can visit them. They try to keep their country not being messed up by too many tourists from all over the world, just like other big cities. And although it is a small country, they still manage to proportionally plan the whole country with mountains, seas, springs, rivers, plains and national parks, etc. creating an open space for people. I neither like Hong Kong, nor Singapore, because over there, people are squeezing in cramped cages among concrete and high-rise buildings.

My friend, Fong, lives in an apartment on 3rd floor near Taipei 101. Fong was from another city. He came to Taipei for study and work. After graduating, he spent a couple of months in the USA then backed to Taipei to open his own business making electric skateboard. Fong is young, passionate, enthusiastic, and talented but he still saves his mornings to read, meticulously make black coffee or rapidly ride skateboards with nice soars. No matter what he does, the passion lights up in his eyes. Even the way he treated me – a stranger from Vietnam. Actually, it was really easy to find a cheap room to stay during days in this city, just the way I always did before. But, after many trips, I've learnt that having a local friend introduce their culture and their city will give us more knowledge than we expected and that city might become incredibly lovely. I would never forget the breakfast place with only Chinese menu that I couldn't read a single word on it, where the lady smiled at me because I might be her first foreign customer. I would not fail to remember days walking on streets leading to the MRT Station, or when I had to run fast to meet up with someone. It may sound funny but those moments made me feel like I was familiar to the city as much as a local. In one way or another, I close the gap between a traveler and a local. Learn the way locals live, the way they eat, the way they drink, the way they breathe and the way they love their city, that is how I fall in love with the city, in a dear way.

In those days in Taipei, Fong drove me around on his bike, to the Yangmingshan to see the boiling lakes of lava on the volcano peak, to smell the strong scent of Sulphur rising from deep black holes or to drop by a hot spring for a foot bath in the natural hot water with dull red sediment under the stormy weather. I thank Fong for all of those. His enthusiasm encouraged me not to pull back in the rain. He kept on riding his bike with me behind on the slippery road leading to the mountain.

One time, under the rain, Fong asked me:

"Have you ever walked on bare foot?"

"I lived in countryside when I was a kid, I walked with bare foot all the days. Barefoot? It's not a big deal!" I replied.

Ok, so here we went. We hiked along the trail shoeless, stepped on round pebbles, rocks, grass, rain and days of youth. Lana Del Rey was still singing the song "Summer sadness" on the phone. I treasure those moments of my life. The moments that would never ever come back. Under the sky with dark clouds threatening or under the rain pouring heavily on us, we were still walking on bare foots, talking about our plans and dreaming of places, about Taiwan and Vietnam and strange people we met and hard times we went through on the first days we started our businesses. We might have different starts, but the roads we were following were somewhat similar – it was the desire to explore the world or to be in charge of our own lives. I was lucky to find such a good and sensible host like Fong. And then we ended up calling each other "Brothers".

Before that, I didn't really like Taiwan. The impression from confabs like Taiwan men came to Vietnam to buy wives or our labor went there to work in factories, I always thought of Taiwan as a land of industrial zones and countryside families with old men. Against my imagination, Taipei was beautiful and civilized so much that it overwhelmed me while they still continued their time-honored traditional values – temples and pagodas mingling in residential areas, mountains and rivers over the green city. The international community are day by day joining in making Taipei more colourful. I met many friends from Japan, USA, Europe, Australia, etc. and Taiwan who spoke English fluently in a Meetup meeting that Fong once brought me too. Or like Taiwanese I met on the way: Fong who owned a company on 1st floor of a modern designed mall, Che Li owned an e-commerce company, Che Wei wrote business books and lectures in universities, the Japanese Saki from USA who just won a scholarship to study in Shanghai. Th ey were all young and talented. But, it didn't make me feel unconfi dent about myself. On the contrary, I found the motivation to try more. We were born in diff erent countries with diff erent destinies, but there is one common language called COURAGE. As long as we have enough courage to overcome challenges, we are still on the same road.

One night, Fong asked me if I wanted to try riding skateboard back home. It was raining, on and off. I had never tried such so I refused, suggesting I would try later in a dry day and in a park to make sure no car would run into me. That night, I made a promise with Fong: I would come back, one day, just to bring the skateboard to the nearby park, blending in the happy young guys, to live the days of youth…

City view from Victoria Peak, Hongkong

Get lost in Lan Kwai Fong, Hongkong

An old temple in Hongkong

Chinese tea egg along food street, Hongkong

A long day & night in Tokyo, Japan

A ancient Japanese temple in Kyoto, Japan

A park in Tokyo, Japan

A market in Osaka, Japan

Shibuya Crossing on the weekend, Tokyo, Japan

Sagano bamboo forest, Kyoto, Japan

Tiger's nest in the winter, Bhutan

A Bhutan Dzong on the mountain, Bhutan

At a Thanka with a local person, Bhutan

Bhutanese children's smile, Bhutan

A Bhutanese family on the way to Tiger's nest, Bhutan

A Bhutan Dzong on the mountain, Bhutan

Taipei in the sunlight, Taiwan

A corner of Taipei, Taiwan

A foggy Yangmingshan, Taiwan

Chang Kei-Shek Memorial Hall, Taiwan

Jiufen village on a rainy day, Taiwan

PART III

SCRAP NOTES ON
THE ROAD

CHAPTER 10

THINGS THAT HAPPENED
NATURALLY

O ccasionally, I have my mind wander back to things happened at a certain time. They are just sudden memories that if had not been at that moment, they would have forever drifted in drawers of the past. Because they are too minor, too mediocre to be memorized events. I didn't know that, life has been made of such simple little things.

There was a time, in an apartment in Guang Zhou, on a sofa in the middle of a living room, I was sitting at one end, my friend was at the other end. It was eight Celsius degrees outside but it felt like freezing in the room. I wrapped myself in a grey blanket, and my friend was in a green one. TV was showing "I am Singer" – Season 3. Han Hong[15] was singing a song about Father, "dubbed" from Chinese to English by my friend so that I could get the meaning. The

---

15   Han Hong is a Chinese singer and songwriter of mixed Tibetan and Han ethnicity - one of the most popular Chinese female musicians who specializes in a variety of Chinese folk music. Most of her work reflects the Tibetan culture.

lyric was absolutely amazing and I don't think it could get any better than that. And we talked about our intentions, plans, dreams and even crazy things. Then we laughed as if we were close friends long time ago before that. That was all I can remember in that cold winter night, nestling in blankets and speaking a language that was not ours, yet it felt like we knew each other, each word, each sentence...

My friend said: Hey Tam, next time you come, stay longer. I would take you to Tibet, and drive you around. Then I dreamt of Tibet and played a song called "Qing Zang Gao Yuan" (meaning "Tibetan Plateau") – by Li Na. He was really impressed "How can you know this song?". "Well, because I like it." Then the next song was by Alin – one of my favourite Taiwanese singers and thanks to that, I had more to talk with him.

Another day in Taipei, Fong said "let's go out" then he pushed us onto a bus to visit Jiu Feng. I am not going to tell the story of my trip to the famous village – just that it was the day I first met Saki. The weather on that day made me think of the feeling when sitting in a tea house by the cliff, down there was the thick layer of fog, and underneath the fog was the deep great ocean. Suddenly, I thought I need to hear a certain kind of music, so I grabbed the phone and played "Gei wo yi ge li you wang ji" (Give me a reason to forget). Saki was like "hey, you listen to this?" Yeah, why not, I was in Taiwan, right? If not Alin's music, then whose else? Saki sang along and that was the beginning of our endless talks on the way back. I met Saki again in Hanoi, he asked: still listen to Alin? Well, I don't think so! Tam now is listening to some crap music.

Saki is Japanese with Canadian nationality, living in Taiwan and studying Mandarin. I knew Saki via Fong, my friend. Saki was quite a typical Japanese with closed attitude though we had met each other a couple of times before.

I love moments that would never come back. Surely, at that very moment, in that very place, with that very person, it was the most beautiful image that my poor memory can capture, deeply. Like the time in Syracuse, a small town on the way from New York to Niagara Falls, I spent four hours on bus just to play some bowling, to drink some beers and to have a few good laughs with friends, then left. That's it. Nothing more. Seems like we set too many goals for our life, or too many purposes for our deeds – too many to realize that everything happens for a reason. Sometimes, it is good to be carefree, just take it when thing comes, as it should be. And we should be happy, no matter what. Simplifying life, gaining more joy.

Then I recalled the hours sitting with friends on the steps in front of Times Square – New York. I couldn't believe that we could meet each other here, so did May and Tuan. May left for the USA first, went to university then found a job. I also had that dream but it was far far to make it come true. I always said to her "I will try to follow you". But New York is more overreached than a dream. Tuan is a friend I knew in Saigon. Yet, we met up here, in the middle of the legendary Times Square. I stood in front of the building of NYPD (The City of New York Police Department), watching Tuan approaching. We then together walked to Korean Town to meetup with May. Later, we found us back on the steps taking wefies with glistening neon lights were up there overhead. To get there, I took a very long way, literally and figuratively. Long but twinkle… There are moving moments when despite how much we talked and laughed, the emotion was unable to put into words!

Or like when I walked into a coffee shop, trembly turned the first pages of the first book I had ever written, smelt the scent of freshly printed...

Those are things that can't be called event, and can't be remembered. But I have a tiny drawer, just to stock all those "nonsense". In sleepless nights, I would pull open that drawer, flip through each one, to watch my peaceful old days – normal, but silently strong…

CHAPTER 11

LIFE ON BOAT

O ctober 2015, I had a trip from Singapore to Malacca (Malaysia) on a five-star cruise that was likely to be interesting. Attention, five stars! My roommate cancelled the trip at the last minutes, so I had the whole room for myself, on 4th floor. Not sure if it was lucky or not, yet I am missing those days drifting aimlessly by the water through the porthole of the cruise.

I didn't imagine that the cruise ship would be so huge before I really saw it. If I remember correctly, it had 8 floors, with two swimming pools on the rooftop. The inner elevators were busy days and nights. The casino was always packed at any time of the day. It didn't matter what time it was when you were on the ship. There were only times when you got crazy in that closed space with the same faces walking on the same stairs eating in that same dining places. Everything was a circle that was so tight that we felt so suffocated in it.

One morning, I woke up, idly stared out the ocean, seeing the water pounding the ship in the chilly room which surely couldn't be as comfortable as a hotel room on land. After lazily planning what to do during the day, I wrapped myself in a towel and walked to farthest swimming pool to lay back into the water. There were a Singaporean couple swimming slowly. We had thought it would be the quietest but we figured out we were wrong when a group of Indians arrived and plunged into the small pool. I quickly jumped out and sat on the edge. The Singaporean couple also swam to the stair to climb out of the pool and wrapped themselves in the big towels. Well, yeah, that was fine, enjoy the surroundings then.

"Enjoy the surroundings" was the most luxury verb in this cruise. Because there was one and only thing: water – the deep blue ocean. No trees, no houses, nothing. Only the water floating and the ship was like staying still. I kept walking around, taking photos and seeing the same people I had seen the whole time as a cycle. Well, what else I can do. On this nobody-in-nobody-out ship, slowing down was the only right I had.

Even so, if being asked "was it beautiful?", my answer would be "Yes, it was beautiful." In mornings at dawn, the sun slowly climbed up in the east. Or in evening at sunset, he sank in the west sky over the waves creating an extraordinary scene.

I met some young Vietnamese boys and girls working on the ship. Some worked in restaurant, some worked as dealers in the casino, some were room service. I sometimes engaged them in short conversations just to receive a same response: "It's boring here. Not as lively as on land". Yeah, it was really boring. My mind felt like dried up after only some days stuck around here. I felt as if I belonged to nowhere. Everything was floating, vague and not clear. It was funny that when I was young, I used to dream to work on five-star cruise ships to travel the world. I had never known that I would see nothing but water if travelling the world this way.

There were insomnia nights, I went up on the deck to hang out with colleagues when stars already filled up the wide night sky. There was absolutely no sound around and it made nights become too quiet with the ship siren made a howling sound from time to time then disappeared in the darkness. People might think it was romantic. But I could feel a bit slack. Solitude – it was the solitude that filled up the space. No one said a word, and someone made a sigh…

I don't know. I needed an anchor, not this insecurely fixed feeling. And when I looked into the eyes of young boys and girls on the ship, I saw the desire to earn enough money to go home. Or to anywhere they want to, but it must be some land with streets, vehicles, families and friends. They had enough water, day by day pounding into the ship. Morning, afternoon or evening, seems like it doesn't matter anymore. It was just days idly passing by outside the picture windows.

Until the day I left the ship, there was no knowing yet of where those days might sweep off to…

CHAPTER 12

I HAVE DATE WITH WINTER

Without an appointment, I was always in somewhere cold during winter in recent years. Two years ago, I was in Europe watching first snows in Paris. Last year, I spent a long winter in the USA while crossing from East coast to West coast. This year, though telling myself to find a warm place to close the year, I eventually ended up in China when the sky already turned grey and people tried to avoid the cold wind by pulling up sweater collars to cover their neck.

Someone asked me if I love winter. No, hell No. While some of my friends wished to have chance to know what winter was like, I was scared. Maybe because my health would not be able to handle it, or maybe because I already got too familiar with the warm sunshine in Saigon. Every single time strolling through streets, I just wanted to complain "it is too cold for anyone".

Though the title "I have date with Winter" sounds kinda romantic, those dates didn't happen for any romantic purpose. Two years ago, I bought ticket to fly to Europe on Lunar New Year's Eve day just because the price couldn't be any lower – no one would fly on that day of the year. As for last year, I planned to see the world's largest Christmas tree in New York. It must be the one at Rockefeller Center otherwise the motivation would be zero. I made it! To the freezing cold East coast with Washington D.C, New York City, Philadelphia, and Boston; then to the windy West Coast with sunny California. There were nights I felt asleep with terrible headache or mornings when we opened the car door just to see a frozen bottle of water. If that was meant to be a date, pretty sure it was not a romantic date.

Notwithstanding, I never imagine that one day I would moan with friends that... I miss the bone-chilling coldness and huddling myself while walking on streets.

I miss the feeling of wearing layer and layer of clothes, gloves and socks without knowing how the chilling wind still could go inside the body.

I miss the hot shower water that quickly became cold by the time it reached legs.

I miss even those leaves, park benches, and faces that all turned cold.

Nostalgia is weird. It is unnecessarily something tender and sweet to be remembered. Sometimes, our mind records those that we experienced and didn't want it to happen again. Human memory works in an unexplainable way. And my sudden nostalgia for the winter cold is such an example.

Regardless of my guess that I would fail to keep the annual date with winter, there is always a thing called destiny – what is meant to be will always find its way. Last days of the year, when half of winter had already past, and no plan for any trip was made, I found myself standing in front of the Embassy of China to apply for visa under the Saigon heat. Having experience, I didn't want myself to suffer from the coldness of Beijing or Shanghai, I chose Guangzhou and Shenzhen for the solo trip. The weather forecast said it was only 16 – 18 degree over there, so it should be fine. However, I still prepared warm clothes just to be sure – heavy luggage of sweaters, gloves and socks. I thought they were just contingency.

But they helped, actually. One day while I was eating in a restaurant, I realized I was the one who was wearing the most clothes. Everybody else was wearing light stuff. The next day, I decided to wear light. Then I was not sure if it was getting colder or I already got sick. My friend said it was colder than the previous day, the temperature dropped some degrees. That "some degrees" was enough to make me feel shivered. I had to run back to the hotel just to get more clothes. There were days at 14 degrees but down to 10 at night, not to mention showers at midnight.

It is said that warm lands wish to be cold lands. But too cold would be inconvenient. Every activity would be affected, from travelling to taking shower and doing laundry. Every morning, it always gave me shock whenever I put my feet down to get out of the bed because of the cold ground. Whenever it was time to take a bath, I played the brain struggle "shower or not shower". Or when walking along street and being hit by the cold "romantic" wind, it was really annoying. However, the worst was clothing. It was cold outside, and warm inside. So, every single time entering and leaving a place, I had to repeat putting on and taking off. I doubt that the locals spent their half-life just to put on and take off clothes?

Well, it seems like I can spend the whole day telling bad things about winter. But inside of my heart, there seems to be different, as if I has already saved a place in my heart for it. There will always be times that I miss the feeling of being alone in a coffee shop to enjoy a hot coffee and to read a book until the last page, or times when I held a Starbucks cup of hot drinks just to warm my hands while walking around some quarters, or feelings of excitement watching the breath disappearing in the air, or the heart skipping a beat when running my hand into other's pocket, or just a quiet moment sitting in the park watching people passing by.

I usually remember nonsense things. They just float and float in my mind. Then suddenly, intentionally or unintentionally, every year, when Saigon is hit by a cold wind making the weather cooler and gentler, I pack my stuff and leave for a certain city, just to complain every day that "it's damn cold here". Missing Winter seems to be an untitled nostalgia...

Winter in Guangzhou was just like winter in anywhere else, just like Winter in Europe or USA, they are all cold. The difference may just be the location of my dates with Winter, when I throw myself out there to enjoy the bone-chilling coldness and romantic sadness, then left my mind strolling along the corners of memory. Seemed like leafless roads of winter would be a stop for me after leaving in the burning heat of Saigon. All to create a balance for me, to create new ideas, new energy.

CHAPTER 13

HANOI IN AUTUMN, TINGED WITH COLOURS OF ELDER TREES...

There were autumn nights when I just simply took a stroll on the promenade around the Hoan Kiem Lake [16] and listened to the famous songs about Hanoi, trying to melt myself into the surroundings. Everything – the weather, the atmosphere, the song, and the smell of "Hoa sữa" (milkwood pine flower) – was brought together as one thing that people called "the autumn of Hanoi" – the elegance that no one can ignore.

The motorbike driver at the junction near the hotel smiled at me and asked "you stay there?", pointing to the hotel. I replied "Yes, it's company benefit for business trip". "Then you should take a taxi, huh" He asked. "Well, yeah, but it doesn't matter, I just want to enjoy the fresh air". It was a 5-star hotel. But... it didn't make a difference, right? A fancy hotel or a dirty small room somewhere on the way, it

---

16   *Hoan Kiem Lake is a fresh lake in the historical center of Hanoi, the capital of Vietnam. Hoan Kiem means "returning the sword". According to the legend, it was the site where the Dragon King reclaimed the sword he had given Emperor Le Loi to fight against Chinese.*

doesn't matter. I am alone, eventually. To me, loneliness is just the same anywhere...

One time, after taking my "Hanoi walk", I went to Hapro[17] for an ice-cream. Initially, I intended to ask a friend to join but my phone died of empty battery. Well, didn't matter. I would just enjoy myself in the relaxing atmosphere and watch people. There were so many beautiful things to see: a girl sitting opposite holding a white puppy, an old couple here, some tourists there. Over the lake, on the other side, the building of Hanoi Post Office still had lights on, so did Tháp Rùa (Turtle Tower [18]). If the phone had not died, I would have taken many photos, that's for sure. But without it, I would capture them all with my memory. I believe that things happen for a reason, surely. The fact that I couldn't use my phone freed me more and made me comfortable – to enjoy the cold ice-cream, to get the gently breeze blowing from the lake, to catch the smell of milky flowers around the place. They were here, and now.

I had many memories with this Hapro. Long time ago... like many years ago... I usually sat here when I was sad, until late at night, no matter what season – autumn or summer, or even in freezing winter. Sometimes with friends, sometimes without friends. There were also times when it can't be any colder and breaths came out as smoke. Yet, I didn't leave. I still sat there, played the ice-cream

---

17 Hapro Bon Mua Coffee : a coffee kiosk just next to Hoan Kiem Lake, offering an excellent view. It's a place where locals and tourists would come, chitchat, sip leisurely a beer, look at the lake and enjoy the atmosphere and watching people.

18 Turtle Tower: the tower was erected on the Turtle islet, in the middle of Hoan Kiem Lake. This is the former fishing site under King Le Thanh Tong period. This nearly-150-year-old tower is a symbol of patriotic pride for the people of Hanoi.

challenge with Thủy. I was too young then, and childish, and overthinking...

Tonight, it was incredibly beautiful regardless of the shower that morning after an overnight rain. I joked with colleagues "So, every time I visit Hanoi, the weather is always this kind of condition. Haizza, so sad!" Maybe the God listened to my complaint? That was why in the last night of the trip, it became quite pleasant. Taxi was not my choice anymore. I decided to take a walk (of course, motorbike taxi should be the option if the distance was too long to walk).

I sat down by the lake for quite a long time, long enough to fill my lung with the smell of autumn. Then I strolled back to the hotel, not too far, about 15 minutes away only. But that fifteen minutes was like a full tour of Hanoi: bustling streets and pavements with ancient smell, young faces under the flickering shadows of trees that you can't mistake with anyone else but "Hanoian", street coffee places that never became old-fashioned. There must be many generations that passed by this corner. It was still there... patient, humble and quiet... I would have had missed these things if my phone hadn't died. I would have glued my face into the phone, checking Facebook, replying messages, listening to music. I felt thankful because my phone did not distract me so that I had chance to watch the people, the streets, the coffee places, the corners, the exciting noise from the kids doing dragon dancing waiting for the mid-autumn festival... It was like the autumn was slipping through my fingers... I saw days of youth passing by this street. I would remember all. Even a very tiny funny memory when Dong warned me "I am wearing 4 layers of clothes and still feeling cold" but I didn't believe him and laughed hard; yet eventually, I shamed myself texting him "I am wearing 7".

I used to drive at a rattling pace on Ba Trieu street, Hue street, or Giai Phong street. But this time, things changed a lot, so much that when my taxi passed by the same street, I felt doubtful "Is it?". Like the night before, Duy and Nhung brought me to eat goat hot pot. The moment we got off, I asked "Is it the Trade Union University?" It looked so, but I was not sure. The surroundings were so different. Surprisingly, it really was. I used to live just the opposite, straight into the small alley. After working, I went to the gym just next to the university. Quang was just a junior then, but now, he already had kids. Streets changed a lot, I didn't have enough confident to drive fast.

Hanoi is modest, at least, in my memory. I would leave the day after. How long would autumn stay here? But that night, I just wanted to be alone, in this cool weather, strolling along streets I used to be, sitting in the place I used to sit, thinking about people I used to meet, and seeing myself getting older. Time passed by and created a separation. Occasionally, I saw some faces on the streets and wondered "Could it be...her?"

CHAPTER 14

———

I AM VIETNAMESE!

F irstly, I would like to quote a sentence posted on Facebook by a friend of mine who is an authentic French named Florent: "Il y a maintenant 1 an, je débarquais au VIETNAM! Entre aventures, découvertes & rencontres de personnes qui ont changé ma vie, c'est une expérience que je ne suis pas près d'oublier! — feeling nostalgic."[19]

While Viet Nam is so much beloved by foreigners, in the eyes of many Vietnamese, it is ugly. Every day, there are still way too many complaints from "netizens" about people, country, etc. Generally speaking, if it is about Vietnamese, it would be "auto-ugly". But, after many many trips, seeing many many things, I have different eyes about what is happening. This is not a Pollyanna-ish sentiment that everything will be just fine. Rather it is a direct look into the matter to see its nature, not an exhorter without a serious analysis.

One winter in Paris, while I was trembling in a big sweater, the puddle on the ground was already froze into ice, my friend

———

19 *Translation: "One year ago, I arrived Vietnam and stayed here for one year already. After all life-changing trips, new things I've learnt and people I've met, I believe this is something I would never forget.*

murmured: "I wish this winter could end soon. Oh, my goodness, I hate winter, I love summer a lot, Tam." I was no better, I was shaking in a line queuing to enter the dining place, but when hearing of summer, I immediately think of Nha Trang. Ooh la, if I were rolling on the white sand beach of Nha Trang, oh man…! I whispered to him "Do you know that it's all year-round summer in my country?" He turned his head "NO WAY". C'mon, there can't be no where on earth with summer all year long. I winked at him and smile: "there is such place – Vietnam. And for your information, beaches in my country are super beautiful." And I spent that whole night telling him about Vietnam and some other Southeast Asian countries with endless summer.

My friend, he never travelled to Asia. He thought there were 4 seasons everywhere. And winter was typically interminable with the snowy sky, stripped trees and the shivering coldness. I felt so awesome, because I successfully stirred his pain of being cold. He said to me with the eyes lit up "Tam, I want to visit Vietnam".

Indeed, people usually like things they don't have. And one more truth: "Travel broadens the mind". The more I travel, the more I see how small I am in front of this big world. Before going out of the country, I had thought it was the same everywhere. But later, I learnt facts, like in winter days can get dark at 4pm and in summer, sun still shines at 9 pm. I heard that it can be much later in the middle of summer. There are even places where the sun doesn't set. Or another fact: say… now it is summer in most places in the world, huh? But in Australia, they start their cold winter. I believe that not everyone in this world knows that Vietnam is a special country with the North is awfully cold while the South is like burning. Or not all would know about the image of two different weathers separated by the Trường Sơn Đông and Trường Sơn Tây [20] – one sunny, the other rainy.

The topic of our endless summer is always a "saviour" for me when chitchatting with foreign friends. They felt interested in things they had never experienced. And I'm pretty sure that they all want to lie out on the beach drinking coconut under the tropical sunshine. You don't like it? then I don't know what kind of creature you are, haha (joking)

Long time ago, when first going abroad, I did feel a bit nervous with my Vietnamese passport (well, yeah, shame on me, huh!?). I was acquired crap thinking like "Vietnamese passport would not pass Singaporean immigration" "Thailand police would check Vietnamese more seriously" or "USA airport would reject your entry", blah blah blah... I honestly didn't know anything, always had fear of treatment discrimination. Yet later, I travelled all over, far and wide. And to my surprise, I have always been fairly and warmly treated. I think "We are what we think" – if I consider myself a criminal, I would look like a criminal, if not, then I am not and I am entering their country confidently – to travel, to explore, to learn and to shop. Even when I travelled to powerful countries (like France, USA, Japan, etc.), I was extra proud of being a Vietnamese. In their eyes, Vietnam is still a poor country, "then how can you manage to travel here, not to mention that you are alone?". Replying to them, I said "Vietnam

---

20   Literally translated: East of the Long Mountains and West of the Long Mountains.

is changing. It's so different now already. No war and young people are travelling around the world. I'm not the only one."

Of course, I said that with a proud face, not only of me, but also of the whole generation. We are young, we work hard, we can speak English, we love travelling, we don't feel strange when connecting with the world. Then, we are already international citizens. Who said only people from rich countries can travel and experience? Who said people holding Vietnamese passport should be cringing?

Forget it! All the tabloids that said about "ugly Vietnamese" just deserve being thrown in trash. In every society, there are always both good and bad, this kind or that kind of people. If I am not confident, then I am already a loser, understandably.

One time, in Paris, I was talking to Julia's dad. He had been settled in France for so long already that he can't remember when, yet he still speaks Vietnamese fluently. He said "It's full of nuts here, kid. They speak French anytime and said they are French. They refused to be Vietnamese. But what kind of French that has dark hair, brown skin and flat nose? It is just a citizenship while your whole thing is obviously Vietnamese. No matter what citizenship you are holding, it is an undeniable fact! We are Vietnamese, until death.

He spoke up a fact that he observed in that community. Not because he loved Vietnam a lot, or because he hated those people. But I agreed with him, if someone denies their origin then where do they belong to? I-am-Vietnam. And I can travel to everywhere in the world (if I try to). And I proved myself. I did tell you my other story, right? About the time I applied for the USA visa. I have just a small amount in bank account, yet I was granted the visa. Why? Because I made them believe that if I ever want to stay there, I definitely can exist in that society without being a burden of their government. Later, many people asked why they failed the USA visa even when they have billions of dollars? Money is just a part of the thing, it's not all. There are more criteria. If they are not qualified, they failed, simply.

Then the Taiwan story. Everybody knows that Vietnamese labor in Taiwan is a big population, they came there to work in factories and in households as helper. That time, I flew in Taiwan from The USA with China Airlines. I made use of the transit duration to have some hours visiting Taipei. But things are not always what we expected. When I arrived, they didn't let me out of the airport. I figured out later that I must fill in an online form in advance, and have it printed in order to leave the airport. I did ask them for support but they were quite unfriendly and said "We can't help". Can't help!? Why? They were actually helping a white traveler. Because I am having Vietnamese passport? I pondered for a while then moved to another terminal, straight entered the China Airlines area and seriously told them "I wanted to go into the city. I would appreciate your service if you provide me the required paper so that they let me out." The staff looked at each other and then quickly processed my request. They really made an effort to provide what I want. I didn't care what they thought about me being a Vietnamese or about the Vietnamese passport, I just want them to learn how to respect a Vietnamese. Even if I were a worker, then what that unfriendliness and unhelpfulness means, huh? Asking for this kind of help is my right, not a mercy that I have to beg them for. Even if they say No to me, they should have proper attitude.

After the airport, I booked a free tour into the city, then again, I received a weird look by the staff after she saw my passport. "We finished. No more seat." She said. Oh Fine, I can do it myself. It would be OK if the white person that came after me still can book a ticket for the tour. Or maybe he already pre-booked? But, whatever. I just gave up on them and went to the next counter to buy city bus to do the tour on my own.

I just wanted to say that, in any case, don't ever self-convince that we are treated badly because we are Vietnamese. Should always remember that we are customers, we are human, we deserve fair treatment. No matter what nationality we are, Vietnamese, Singaporean, Thais, Laos, Cambodia, it should not be a problem. I come here legally, I have freedom in behavior and, I don't do anything wrong and don't violate any laws, therefore I don't deserve the discrimination. That is the way of thinking. I believe we should not make it a barrier to be fretful. It should not be a way to protect yourself because it's not even something to be protected. Don't think it as an unfairness (although Bill Gates said "Life is unfair", he didn't mean that being born as Vietnamese would be unfairly treated as an obvious fact). Again, you are what you think. If you think you are already a loser being born as Vietnamese, then you are really loser. If you change your perspective, think it's just a common unreasonable treatment and it is just your bad luck to show up in a bad day of someone, then it's not the fault of being a Vietnamese. Most of the time, I am a super friendly guy, and I proudly say "I am Vietnamese". Trust me, I was treated well many times also, and I didn't have to deny my identity.

Yet, sometimes I heard about stories of "national shame". It sounds weird, right? It's a new word, new concept in Vietnam – before, people were shameful for themselves only. Like the news about Vietnamese thieves in Japan, having buffet in Singapore, stealing in Thailand, or illegal immigration in Korea, etc. all those kinds of news made us feel shameful on behalf of the whole nation. One time, when I was going to travel to Japan, someone said "Be careful because Japanese hate Vietnamese". I corrected him "You are so wrong. Japanese quite like Vietnamese. And they are smart enough to know that those bad cases can't be representative for the whole community of Vietnamese who are working hard and diligently in Japan or for the whole country of Vietnam who are nice and kind. Strangely, the Japanese I've met love Vietnam. They had travelled to Vietnam, to Ha Long Bay and Saigon. Some told me excitedly that they were going to travel to Vietnam. They complimented on the hospitality of Vietnamese. I was not surprised hearing such. I know my people. Vietnamese always tried to help whenever possible. They tell each other stories of Vietnamese kindness, and they believe that it would be fun travelling to Vietnam and there are many nice people in Vietnam.

But there are robberies in Vietnam! Well, even Vietnamese suffer that social evil. It was no surprise that tourists are robber's preys because they don't even spare for locals. They would not stop to judge if you are Vietnamese or tourists just to save the national prestige. They are robbers, they rob for living. That's it. That kind of information is easily to find on the internet. I am sure that every tourist knows that before they travel to Vietnam and they would protect themselves.

I asked a friend of mine "Are you afraid of robbery?" He said "Well, that makes it interesting". He prepared himself and get ready to be robbed but eventually (or luckily), robbers missed him. And that made him proud. And it is this complicated society that give foreign tourists the sense of differences – every country has its own problems. And those differences create the diversity of the world. And talking about differences, Vietnam has a lot to offer – it is like another world that Westerner would not imagine. Many people choose to stay here to live, to work and to be happy in their own way. I don't get the issue that while there are many people from all over love Vietnam, many locals see their own country as a land of ugliness and dirtiness and they just dream of fleeing from it. To change a society and its problems, we need time and patience. Can't be rush. Sadly, patience is something that many of us are lack of…

I was told a shocking story that Westerners backpackers share each other: if they spend all money they have on the way, just sell phones, laptops or cameras to get some money, then report a robbery to the police, obtain certificate stating that they are robbed in Vietnam to claim insurance or get a new one (phone, for example). Those tricks are evils. We Vietnamese would believe that they lost on the way of travelling in Vietnam because that practice does happen, and we felt pity for them as well as shame on us. But from what I learnt, I also believe that people are not that naïve. Most of travellers travel to Southeast Asia in general and Vietnam in particular would buy insurance for themselves and if they don't have enough sense of security to protect themselves and go to places where even I myself can't protect me, then who to be blamed? Of course, everybody wants a better society. But before it gets better, let's learn how to live with it and consider that an experience.

Living with it, sometimes, is a good thing. Before arriving Vietnam, most of Westerners prepare for themselves an interesting trip. Either beautiful or ugly, it should be interesting; because they have never ever experienced such and pretty sure that Vietnam is a must-discover country that people need to spend time with it. There are not many countries with favorable conditions like Vietnam, to be honest. We have gorgeous beaches along the country, diversified great food and cultures in different regions, dozens of ethnic groups living together in peace. My foreign friends love to ride motorbike from Da Nang to Hue to enjoy the beautiful landscape, to float lanterns in Hoi An, to walk in the Old Quarter of Ha Noi, to travel Sapa to listen to the mountains breathing, to sunbath in Nha Trang and Mui Ne, to party hard in sleepless Saigon or to enjoy peaceful cool days in Da Lat and beautiful Cải lương[21] (Renovated theatre) in Mekong Delta.

Before, I used to bring my foreign friend to see the Notre Dame, the Opera House, the Post Office building because I believed

---

21   Cai Luong (Renovated Theatre), a theatre form created by Southerners in Vietnam, is the confluence of cultural elements within the country as well as across its border, along the history of the Southern land.

they were special things in my city. Later, when I had chance to visit Europe, it turned out to me that I was so naïve because their cathedrals, and post offices and opera houses are much more massive and stunning than what we have in Saigon. What they need is not to see those architectures but to sit on a motorbike riding along the streets, to squeeze in local markets where sellers are aggressive but immediately change to be nice and kind if buyers are foreigners. They would love to walk along old streets and hear about our history in our own thinking. It is simple, they are looking for what they don't have. Like my friend, Damiano. He always makes me nervous every time I ride him out to the street. Because he would keep on shooting and recording with his phone. I have to remind him many time "Be careful, man!" He put the phone back into the pocket, but take it out again just after some minutes. He is just so excited about Vietnam. But who wouldn't?

One time, I was at Starbucks with a friend, we were reading and working. A couple of tables from us, there were two Korean pretty girls chatting quite loudly. People looked at them but seemed like they were too excited that they don't sense the surrounding. My friend stepped up to and suggested them to lower their voice. Now they got the problems and excused. I believe code of behavior conduct is what everybody should learn before they go out to the society. Vietnamese is friendly and generous, but sometimes noisy. But we are not noisy at any time and we don't make ourselves at home anywhere. So do foreigners. If noisy, they would be reminded.

It's ridiculous if we put on stylish clothes but forget how to behave politely. I'm saying this to tell a fact that no matter which nationality you are, Vietnamese or not, there are always different kinds of people.

We can't stereotype. And because of that, I felt a bit self-offended when travelling to Singapore.

In Singapore, at some buffet places, they have reminders saying "Pick enough that you can eat" – and it is in Vietnamese only. I used to feel bad about it and was angry at my own fellowmen. I thought they were a national shame. The people who make Singaporean have that reminder even don't know what they did wrong, they don't even know why their eating make the whole nation embarrassed. In my country, in my culture, we always cook more than we eat. In our kitchen, there are always food. No matter how poor we are. We want to make sure that whenever we have guests, we have food for them. We save food for neighbours, for close friends who might come over at any time or simply for their kids, who knows if they get hungry mid-day. We can't stand it when the dish is empty, not for ourselves, but for others. That is our hospitality.

That habit can't be unlearnt after some days. Travelling is not for only rich people anymore. It's for everybody. Aunties Uncles in countryside now can also travel. Then they are told that they can eat all food for a set price. And they really "eat all". They go in the restaurant, put as much as possible on the plates with the thinking that "either me or others would finish this", some even think they can bring home some for late night hunger – but they are not allowed. Therefore, I believe that behind all negative stereotypes, there are always a misunderstanding somewhere somehow. And I feel sympathy for such because they are misunderstood and they even don't know how to explain. (of course, there is still a part of bad people who really shame the whole nation and I'm not gonna defense for such.)

In a same society, people have different ways to grow up. And being kind is a choice. Good or bad, it's not the fault of society, so don't blame it. Some people just take good for themselves "I do it on my own" but if bad, they would say "it's not my fault, it's society's fault". That's funny, huh. Nobody can represent for the whole society, you are representative for yourself only. If one thinks this society is not good enough, that it has so many bad things, then try to flee away, find something good for you. Or if you are braver, change it! Don't blame, don't complain. Instead, stand up and walk away and be an example for the good that you are searching for. That is how you contribute for Vietnam, that is how we make Vietnam a better place. Choice is yours, and choice is you.

A small village of Vietnam

An ancient town, Hoi An, Vietnam

St. Joseph's Cathedral, Hanoi, Vietnam

Beside Hoan Kiem lake, Hanoi, Vietnam

A beautiful landscape, Moc Chau, Vietnam

Cruise by the bay, Ha Long Bay, Vietnam

Ha Long Bay, Vietnam

CPSIA information can be obtained
at www.ICGtesting.com
Printed in the USA
LVHW040347180920
666458LV00001B/169